S0-AFK-294

WILLIAM K. KERSHNER

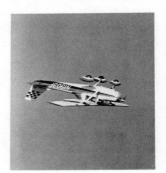

THE BASIC AEROBATIC MANUAL

AILERON ROLL

THE

IOWA STATE UNIVERSITY PRESS

AMES, IOWA

BASIC
AEROBATIC
MANUAL
WILLIAM K. KERSHNER

William K. Kershner started his aerobatic career in a Boeing-Stearman N2S at age 17 and instructed aerobatics and towed banners in a Meyers OTW biplane at 19. At this writing he has over 2000 hours of aerobatic instructing and 2100-plus spins in the C-150/152 Aerobat. Kershner operates a one-airplane, one-instructor aerobatic school in Sewanee, Tennessee, using a Cessna 152 Aerobat. He also is author of THE STUDENT PILOT'S FLIGHT MANUAL, THE ADVANCED PILOT'S FLIGHT MANUAL, THE INSTRUMENT FLIGHT MANUAL, THE FLIGHT INSTRUCTOR'S MANUAL, and coauthor of THE STUDENT PILOT'S STUDY GUIDE.

© 1987 Iowa State University Press
Ames, Iowa 50010
All rights reserved

Manufactured in the United States of America

No part of this book may be reproduced in any form or by any electronic or mechanical means, including information storage and retrieval systems, without permission in writing from the publisher, except for brief passages quoted in a review.

First edition, 1987
Second printing, 1988
Third printing, 1988
International Standard Book Number 0–8138–0063–3
Library of Congress Catalog Card Number 86–083134

C O N T E N T S

PREFACE

THIS MANUAL was written to be used as a reference guide in conjunction with an introductory aerobatic course, with emphasis on flying the Cessna Aerobat. The airspeeds and techniques are those recommended for the Aerobat; however, the maneuvers described may be done (at the appropriate airspeeds) in other airplanes certificated for aerobatics.

The maneuvers are introduced in the expected order of difficulty. You should study the text and illustrations both before and after the flight in which the maneuver is introduced by your instructor.

While we're on the subject of your instructor, it should be noted that self-taught aerobatics is *not* the way to go. That method is certainly very inefficient—and can be dangerous.

This is a guide only. Performance of the various aerobatic maneuvers depends on the experience and skill of the individual, and the time necessary to learn the various maneuvers will vary among pilots. Your instructor will know when you're ready to move on to a new or more complex maneuver.

This book is an updated version of the Cessna 150 *Aerobat Training Manual* written in 1969. The recommended entry airspeeds were in miles per hour rather than knots (which are now almost universally used in flying). Power (rpm) settings were higher than those used in the Cessna 152 Aerobat (the "standard" power setting at cruise for chandelles, wingovers, lazy eights, and aileron rolls is 2300 rpm for the C-152 and 2500 rpm for the C-150 model). The 1976 and 1977 Cessna 150 Aerobats changed to knots but used the same power settings as the earlier 150. I have included speeds and power settings for all models of the airplanes; the first figures are for the C-152 Aerobat in knots, the figures following in parentheses for the C-150 in miles per hour. You'll note that the values don't always jibe with the conversion factor for knots and miles per hour. There are a couple of reasons for this: (1) I have slightly changed some entry speeds (knots) for various maneuvers, based on several hundred hours of instructing in the Aerobat, and (2) the speeds in miles per hour are rounded off to the nearest 10 mph for easier handling in flight. In short, if your Aerobat airspeed indicator is in *knots* use the first recommended speed. If it's marked in *mph,* use the recommended speed given in parentheses.

The maneuvers here cover the general range of g forces from +4.0 to 0 (briefly), and the majority of them can be done within a range of +3.5 to +0.5g's. The stock Aerobat does not have an inverted fuel or oil system, and I believe that the average person should be introduced to the idea of aerobatics in a comfortable environment with no engine power loss or hanging on the belt and harness. Certainly those serious about continuing aerobatics should get further instruction in an airplane that allows the extended negative g's necessary for the performance of more complex maneuvers. Certain maneuvers covered here in an across-the-board introduction to basic aerobatics may not be listed for a particular airplane.

I worked with Joyce Case, Jim Kemper, and Ed McKenzie of Cessna in writing the original training manual in 1969 and thoroughly enjoyed being associated with them.

I would like to thank Jim Bryan, who flew aerobatics with me and took a series of pictures throughout several maneuvers that allowed me to accurately illustrate various instrument indications.

My son Bill, a CFI, helped with data taking on several flights in the Aerobat, noting the times and altitudes required for various maneuvers.

Thanks to Eleanor Ulton for the good typing and automatic correction of grammar and punctuation errors.

Cessna Aircraft Company has kindly given me permission to rewrite the manual as a personal project and has furnished the original drawings and layouts. Since this book is a different and personal approach it should be understood that it is not a Cessna project or an official view by that company.

You won't be anywhere near ready for competition or airshow aerobatics after this course, but this training will increase your confidence and all-around ability to fly *all* airplanes.

Bill Kershner

THE
BASIC
AEROBATIC
MANUAL

1

INTRODUCTION TO AEROBATIC FLIGHT

ADVANTAGES OF AEROBATIC TRAINING

In recent years, flight training in the United States has gradually moved away from the idea of being able to fly the airplane in steeper pitch and bank attitudes. In fact, some professional pilots would be at a loss to know what to do if the airplane exceeded certain pitch or bank limits. Under the current system of certification some flight instructors have never been in a developed spin but have been signed off by a fellow instructor after a one-turn "spin" in each direction, both participants more than glad to terminate the exercise at that point and descend the 10,000 ft back down to the airport.

Many flight instructors are seriously concerned about what they would do in the event of a spin or inverted flight occurring because of a student's, or wake turbulence, action. *Every flight instructor should have at least 5 hours of aerobatic training.* While we're talking about wake turbulence, don't think that *any* amount of aerobatic training and experience would guarantee recovery from wake turbulence on takeoff or landing, but it would give you a *better chance* at recovery at higher altitudes. The aerobatically trained pilot will roll the airplane upright if inverted by wake turbulence or other factors, minimizing the altitude loss, as compared to the pilot without aerobatic training who would most likely pull through a split S (half loop), losing 1000 ft or more. Again, though, *aerobatic training* will not *guarantee* recovery. Wake turbulence should always be respected and feared—and avoided whenever possible.

A second plus for aerobatic training is an added confidence in other phases of your flying. No longer will that great unknown area past 20° pitch and 60° bank be lurking out there waiting to get you. You will expand your envelope of operation for the airplane. There's no real proof, but it's highly possible that as many accidents have been caused by timidity and over-cautiousness as by recklessness; both are usually the result of lack of knowledge and experience in the full approved operating envelope of the airplane. You can

justify the expense of taking an aerobatic course to your spouse by noting that it will make you a safer pilot—which it certainly will.

The third factor is that it will likely be the most enjoyable flying of your career, and this is icing on the cake. It will be challenging as well as enjoyable. (Instrument training is challenging and, for some, enjoyable. Later in this book it will be shown that some aerobatic maneuvers such as aileron rolls, loops, and spins may be done under the hood while your instructor acts as safety pilot.)

As was noted in the Preface, no aerobatic maneuvers should be attempted without first having received dual instruction from a qualified aerobatic instructor. You didn't read a how-to-fly book, jump in an airplane, and teach yourself to get the machine off the ground and back again. This manual assumes that you have a private certificate so the basics of how to turn, climb, glide, and fly straight and level won't have to be reviewed.

The course recommended here will consist of six lessons for a total of 5 hours flight time (see the syllabus at the back of the manual). You can set your own pace in going through the course; however, three flights a day should be your maximum.

You shouldn't try to cram the course through in, say, one day because your rate of learning might not be as great if the new information comes too fast; on the other hand if you fly once every 2 weeks, you'll spend a lot of time reviewing the maneuvers covered the last flight. Try to fly at least twice a week (one flight a day is better) and use this manual as a review between flights.

FEDERAL AVIATION REGULATIONS

In any bona fide aerobatic course you will fly in accordance with the Federal Aviation Regulations and following are some points you should consider. Federal Aviation Regulations (FARs) pertaining to aerobatic flying are as follows.

AEROBATIC FLIGHT

No person may operate an aircraft in aerobatic flight—

(a) over any congested area of a city, town, or settlement;
(b) over any open air assembly of persons;
(c) within a control zone or Federal airway;
(d) below an altitude of 1,500 feet above the surface; or
(e) when flight visibility is less than three miles.

For the purposes of this paragraph, aerobatic flight means an intentional maneuver involving an abrupt change in an aircraft's attitude, an abnormal attitude, or abnormal acceleration, not necessary for normal flight.

Parachute Requirements. You and your instructor will wear parachutes while doing aerobatics. The parachutes should be in good condition and within the packing dates required by regulation. There's nothing like discovering after you've bailed out that you're wearing a fifteen-dollar "bargain" that hasn't been repacked since World War II.

Your instructor will show you how to inspect the parachute before wearing it and will make sure that your parachute has been inspected and repacked by a certified rigger within the required time period. Following are the FARs on the subject.

Parachutes and Parachuting

(a) No pilot of a civil aircraft may allow a parachute that is available for emergency use to be carried in that aircraft unless it is an approved type and—

(1) If a chair type (canopy in back), it has been packed by a certificated and appropriately rated parachute rigger within the preceding 120 days; or

(2) If any other type, it has been packed by a certificated and appropriately rated parachute rigger—

(i) Within the preceding 120 days, if its canopy, shrouds and harness are composed exclusively of nylon, rayon, or other similar synthetic fiber or materials that are substantially resistant to damage from mold, mildew, or other fungi and other rotting agents propagated in a moist environment; or

(ii) Within the preceding 60 days, if any part of the parachute is composed of silk, pongee, or other natural fiber, or materials not specified in paragraph (a)(2)(i) of this section.

(b) Except in an emergency, no pilot in command may allow, and no person may make, a parachute jump from an aircraft within the United States except in accordance with Part 105 of this chapter.

(c) Unless each occupant of the aircraft is wearing an approved parachute, no pilot of a civil aircraft carrying any person (other than a crew member) may execute any intentional maneuver that exceeds—

(1) A bank of 60° relative to the horizon; or

(2) A nose-up or nose-down attitude of 30° relative to the horizon.

(d) *Paragraph (c) of this section does not apply to—*

(1) Flight tests for pilot certification or rating; or

(2) Spins and other flight maneuvers required by the regulations for any certificate or rating when given by—

(i) A certificated flight instructor; or

(ii) An airline transport pilot instructing in accordance with requirements of this chapter.

(e) For the purposes of this section, "approved parachute" means—

(1) A parachute manufactured under a type certificate or a technical standard order (C-23 series); or

(2) A personnel-carrying military parachute identified by an NAF, AAF, or AN drawing number, an AAF order number, or any other military designation or specification number.

If at any time you should notice the chute you are using has grease or what you think might be corrosive material on it, report it to the instructor right away. It may need to be repacked before being worn again. In addition, a parachute could have been handled by the rip cord and some of the pins moved far enough that inspection would be advisable.

If you are using a backpack parachute, the back cushions of the Aerobat seat have been designed to be easily removed and reversed on the seat frame. If a seat pack is used, remove the bottom cushion from the seat.

Area and Altitude Limitations. As noted earlier, you won't be doing aerobatics over a town or settlement or over an open air assembly of persons. You won't do them on a Federal airway or in a control zone or at an altitude less than 1500 ft above ground level. Remember, this is only a minimum—there is no substitute for altitude following an improperly executed maneuver. Being well above this minimum altitude will let you concentrate on properly completing a maneuver without concern for legal or safety minimums.

Along these same lines, it's *always* a wise move to clear the area before each maneuver or series of maneuvers. Maybe you've complied with all of the FARs, but it makes for a great rate of adrenaline flow to fly over the top of a loop and find youself pointed at a military airplane doing its low-level practice in *your* area. The overhead skylights in the Aerobat will help you in clearing the area, as well as being quite useful for positioning the aircraft during the aerobatic maneuvers. *Use them.*

PHYSICAL CONDITION

You should be in good physical condition and mentally alert. If you have passed an FAA physical, you're in good enough average shape to do aerobatic flying. However, if you have a "bug" or some other temporary problem, you won't be at the peak of mental or physical vigor, no matter what your "average" condition is.

The instructor will begin your introduction to aerobatic flying by limiting the demonstrations of each maneuver to a *minimum* amount of time, allowing you to do the vast majority of the flying. Each maneuver will be fully explained and then demonstrated, and you'll know exactly what to expect. Most people adjust quite rapidly to the attitudes of aerobatic flying, and any early nervousness will be eliminated.

The biggest question in the mind of anyone considering aerobatics is, Will I get sick? In a properly sequenced course the chances of nausea are cut to the minimum, but you can help yourself also.

What and how you eat and drink before a flight can have a great deal to do with your reaction to aerobatics. Avoid any heavy or greasy food before flying. For some people, coffee or soft drinks can also be the instigator of nausea problems.

For your first lesson or two, schedule so that you fly at least a couple of hours after eating. This is better for most people than flying on a full *or* empty stomach.

The big point is that *you* will have to let the instructor know when to break off the session, although your sweating or poor coloring may show that things have progressed further than they should.

Most pilots new to aerobatics are highly enthusiastic after the first few maneuvers (and will probably stay that way), but one of the first manifestations of impending trouble, before any noticeable physical symptoms occur, is a sudden decrease of interest in doing another roll or loop. You aren't nauseated and don't have any real physical symptoms, but would just as soon be doing something else. ("On the whole, I'd just as soon be in Philadelphia.") This is called NSMFA (Not So Much Fun Anymore) and is the point at which you should indicate that it's time to cut it short—physical symptoms are pretty sure to follow if more maneuvers are done. It's always better to go back to the airport early and think you could have done a few *more* maneuvers, than to go back late and wish you'd done *fewer.*

If you are having nausea problems that first or second flight, don't get discouraged; a fair percentage of aerobatic trainees do have minor problems or "loss of enthusiasm" during the first flight or two, but by watching their diet before flying and keeping those flights short, they work their way out of the problem and, on the last few flights, can run a full series of maneuvers without any trouble at all.

A couple of added factors that might help are (1) scheduling in the afternoon for a while if you're having problems on the morning flight (or vice versa) and (2) chewing gum during aerobatics to help keep the stomach occupied. (Don't swallow the gum during a particularly involved maneuver.) The rate of chewing can tell the instructor your excitement index—sometimes the gum will take quite a beating.

One aerobatic instructor, when asked what method he used to cope with airsickness on the first few flights, replied, "I let the trainee fly the airplane until I feel better."

Incidentally, if you have a cold or a sinus problem, perhaps you'd better fly another day because you will be climbing and letting down pretty fast in some of the maneuvers. In any case, let your instructor know if at any time you start feeling a little under the weather, so you can have a few minutes of straight and level flying.

ACCELERATION (g) FORCES

You may have had the word on acceleration forces, or g's, for some time, but still it might be well to review the situation, since a 20°-banked turn might have been the wildest flying you've done lately.

The acceleration discussed here is not the kind you normally associate with drag races but the force that results when you change direction—and this force can result while either flying the airplane or walking. Needless to say, you'll be doing a considerable amount of changing directions during aerobatics and will encounter extra g's plenty of times. Specifically, the forces you'll be most interested in are those acting parallel to the vertical axis of the airplane. Here are some points that you may have forgotten.

While reading this, if you are standing still or sitting in a chair or flaked out in the hammock, you have the normal gravity force of 1 g acting on you. For some people, this force of 1 g is nearly too much and they lie around a lot. (If you are reading this while on a carnival ride, or while being fired in an ejection seat, ignore the first sentence in this paragraph.)

In a constant-altitude, properly coordinated, 60°-banked turn, you and the airplane will be under an acceleration force (load factor) of 2 positive g's (Fig. 1-1).

The 2 g's you experience in the 60°-banked turn are *positive;* that is, they are working on you and the air-

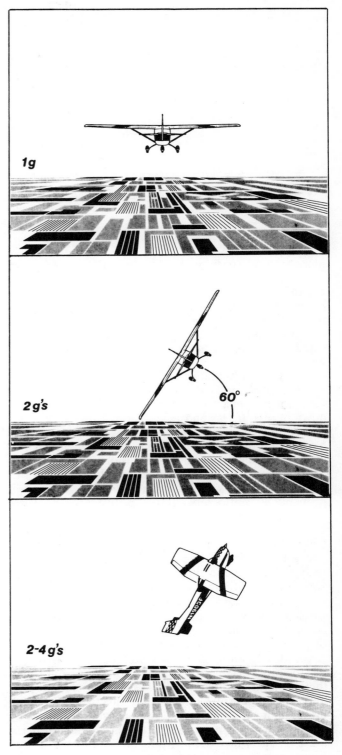

Fig. 1-1. Acceleration forces (g's) in various flight maneuvers.

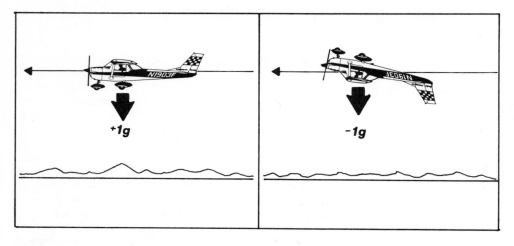

Fig. 1-2. Upright and inverted flight. Because the airfoil of this airplane is not symmetrical, inverted flight requires a higher nose attitude to maintain a constant altitude. Some trainers, including the Aerobat, don't have inverted fuel and oil systems and are therefore restricted in time of inverted flight. (The engine would quit shortly after the airplane assumed the attitude shown in the right half of the illustration.)

plane from top to bottom. The 1 g you are experiencing every day is also positive. However, people who hang around on tree limbs by their legs (with their heads down) have 1 negative g working on them because gravity is working from their feet to their heads. When you and the airplane are flying upside down in steady level flight, you have a 1 negative g working on you (Fig. 1-2).

If you are pulling +3 g's in the airplane (say, in doing a loop), every part of your body weighs 3 times your normal weight and your blood will tend to move down into your legs and feet.

At higher positive accelerations, the draining of blood from the head can cause a grayout (some loss of vision), a blackout (total loss of vision), or finally, loss of consciousness. The maneuvers you'll be doing in this course, however, will not exceed +4 g's and you will probably not notice any effects. For instance, if you are an average pilot, +2 or 3 g's will give you the sense of being firmly pushed in your seat and your hands and feet will feel heavy if you try to move them. At +4 g's you get good evidence that acceleration forces are at work. Things get a little gray if you are relaxed and your cheeks feel like they are sagging.

Wait a minute! The last paragraph said no effects would be likely to be noticed at +4 g's. This is true. The *pilot,* who's doing the flying, doesn't notice the effects of acceleration forces like a passenger does. The pilot is concentrating on the maneuver and may be tensed up a bit; the other occupant, having nothing to do but watch the changing of directions of flight, may start to gray out. The pilot will likely feel no effects at all, which brings up a good point: You can raise your tolerance by tensing up your muscles, particularly your stomach muscles. Navy dive bomber pilots in World War II used to yell as they pulled out of a dive; this tensed the muscles nicely, but probably did nothing for the peace of mind of the gunner, since he was facing backward and couldn't see what was going on.

At about +6 g's the average pilot will have just about no vision and with *extended* time might lose con-

sciousness—but you won't be going to that high a g force in an introductory course.

Negative g's are harder on you than positive g's, and your tolerance will be less. At −2 or −3 g's your face feels full and a headache is in the offing. You are well aware that the seat belt and harness are there (since you are pushing against them). At −4 g's you may literally see red as the brain gets all the blood it needs (and then some). Using the suggested syllabus it's extremely unlikely that you will see less than zero g, or perhaps −0.5 g on your accelerometer. It seems that no matter how tight you think the belt or shoulder harness is before takeoff, when you encounter unexpected negative g's you'll find that it has mysteriously loosened.

The accelerometer, as the name implies, measures acceleration forces (up or down) parallel to the vertical axis of your airplane. Since you are sitting upright in the airplane, it measures the positive- and negative-g forces on you as well. The accelerometer you'll see in the Aerobat is a standard instrument consisting of a spring balance measuring a single weight under varying forces (Fig. 1-3).

Fig. 1-3. Accelerometer.

You'll notice that the instrument has three hands. The "top" hand (or the one closest to the glass) moves with the negative or positive forces being applied at that instant. Under positive-g forces it will move the "middle" hand and leave it at the maximum positive g's pulled in a particular maneuver. With g forces of less than 1 g, the "bottom" (or third) hand is moved and left at the maximum negative reading. After the airplane is returned to 1 g (normal) flight the "top" hand moves back to a 1-g indication and the other hands remain at the maximum positive- and negative-g indications, maintaining a record of the range of forces encountered during a particular maneuver. For instance, you could say, "I pulled a maximum of 4 positive g's and 1 negative g during that series of maneuvers and I see I'm now pulling +2 g's in this 60° turn." A reset button on the instrument is pushed to return the two reference hands back to the normal 1-g reading for another maneuver series.

When the accelerometer is indicating +4 g's, it means you've added +3 g's to the normal 1-g reading. If you've indicated a −2 g's on the instrument, you've gone from +1 g to 0, and then on to −2, which is 3 g's on the negative side of the normal condition.

One thing you'll notice after you have used the instrument is that even in fairly easy pull-ups, such as entering a normal climb, the accelerometer indicates a value greater than +1 g. It may be a very little change and hard to read, but it's there—anytime you change direction of flight up or down.

An interesting note on the effects of g forces on the pilot is that *time* has a lot to do with it. For instance, you may pull +6 or +8 g's by jumping off a chair, but since the time that the g force is being applied is so short, the blood doesn't start to move downward before the force is removed—hence no grayout or blackout. Usually it takes about 3 seconds for such things to get started, so a snap roll, with a +3-g force probably won't even let you realize that you've been under acceleration forces. On the other hand, in a loop where +3 g's are being exerted for a longer period, the "relaxed" pilot (who didn't have any trouble with the +3-g snap roll) may decide that it's getting a little foggy all of a sudden. The airplane is not affected this way because to it +3 g's are +3 g's whether for a short period or a longer time.

Turbulence can add to the load factor. A +3-g maneuver could end up as a +4- or +5-g maneuver if turbulence is encountered at that point. The smoother the air, the better your performance of aerobatics.

You'll find that your positive-g tolerance will increase with experience. Remember, it will be decreased with decreased physical fitness. Low blood sugar (you skipped breakfast altogether) is one factor that may lower g tolerance, and grayouts may happen in maneuvers that didn't bother you on earlier flights.

The Airplane and Load Factors. The Cessna Aerobat is certificated in the Aerobatic category of Part 23 of the Federal Aviation Regulations, for the purpose of aerobatic training. Its limit load factors are +6.0 g's and −3.0 g's; that is, the airplane is designed to withstand these forces without problems during the execution of the maneuvers. More about this later.

The limit load factors (sometimes called flight load factors) are the number of g's (positive and negative) that can be imposed on an airplane without permanent deformation of structure occurring. The ultimate load factors (sometimes called design load factors) are the number of g's (positive and negative) that can be imposed on an airplane without destruction of major components (wings, tail, etc.) occurring. The *ultimate* or *design* load factors must be at least 150% (or 1.5 times) the *limit* (or *flight*) load factors.

In other words, in any airplane, if you exceed the limit (flight) load factors you'll bend the airplane. If you exceed the ultimate (design) load factors you could break the airplane.

The Aerobat and other aerobatic airplanes are specifically designed to be able to safely perform aerobatic flight. Other airplanes you may be flying will likely be in the normal category limit (or flight) load factors (+3.8 and −1.52 g's) and/or the utility category (+4.4 and −1.76 g's) and are not designed or certificated for most of the maneuvers you'll be doing. If you plan to learn how to do the maneuvers in the Aerobat so that you can go out and do them in your normal or utility category Zephyr Six—forget it. You could damage the airplane as well as having an incident report filed on you by the FAA. Familiarize yourself with the aerobatic section of the *Aerobat Information Manual* prior to receiving instruction.

Now that you see the airplane is certificated correctly and have other background information, it's time to do the preflight inspection and get into the air.

THE PREFLIGHT INSPECTION AND PRETAKEOFF CHECK

A thorough preflight inspection is important for any flight, but it takes on added importance for aerobatics. You *might* get by with making a cross-country flight with the oil cap loose or missing (in smooth air) but a slight negative "g" force could clean out the oil sump (and cover the windshield) in very short order. You could end up with an oil-starved engine and an oil-covered windshield—a bad combination, since it's best to be VFR during a precautionary landing. You will probably use the recommended preflight check as given in the *Aerobat Information Manual,* but here are some points you might consider (the steps in the following list are shown in Fig. 1-4, points 1–22):

1. The first step is in the cabin to make sure the ignition is OFF and the control lock has been removed. Turn the master switch ON and fully lower the flaps. (Make sure that the master switch is OFF after the flaps are down.)

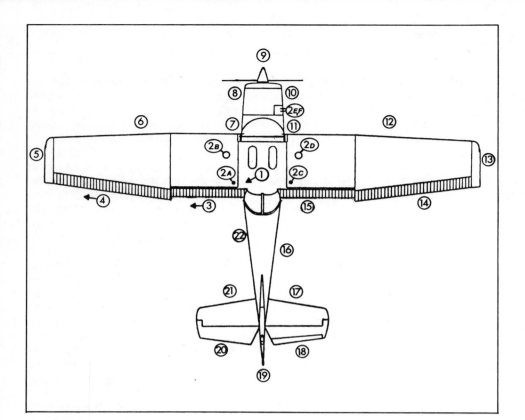

Fig. 1-4. Preflight inspection. This one is set up for the Aerobat but may be used for other airplanes, both aerobatic and non-aerobatic. The numbers indicate particular points of inspection discussed in the text.

2. You may prefer to check fuel and oil as you come to them, but checking the tanks and draining the tanks and fuel strainer to check for water and other foreign material, plus checking the oil, can be done together to avoid missing one of the items. You should make five (5) fuel checks (points *2A-2E*) plus looking at the oil (point *2F*).

Since, with parachutes and two heavy people, the maximum weight could be exceeded if the tanks are full, a wooden (marked) fuel dipstick will come in handy to ascertain the amount of existing fuel or to decide how much to add if it's low. If you are flying a local 1-hour aerobatic flight in fine weather (and it's forecast to remain that way) a 1-hour reserve will be plenty. If you are flying a local solo, particularly on hot summer days, you don't need to carry nearly 5 hours fuel for a 45-minute or 1-hour flight because you'll want the best climb characteristics commensurate with a good reserve if weather makes detouring to other airports necessary. The fuel dipstick is a good aid because very few people can look into a tank and correctly estimate the fuel available (points *2B* and *2D*).

Always drain any fuel into a clear container so that you can hold it up to the light and look for water and other contaminants. This also allows you to confirm that the proper fuel grade is in the system.

If the airplane is being fueled, or has been fueled only shortly before you go out to it, you might want to do the fuel checks after completing the structural check of the airplane. This will give any induced foreign material a better chance to settle to lower levels where it can be drained.

Another point: Drain the wing tanks (points *2A* and *2C*) *before* draining the fuel strainer (the lowest point in the system). If you drain the strainer first, contaminants might be pulled from the tanks down into the lines just far enough to be missed by all three drain points—but in a position to cause problems a little later.

Throughout the following structural check you'll be looking for skin wrinkles and *pulled* or *working* rivets, meaning that the rivet is moving relative to the structure to which it's attached and is no longer the rigid fastener it was designed to be. A working rivet may have a graphite-appearing stain behind or around it and should be brought to the attention of an instructor or mechanic. Even though an aerobatic airplane is stressed for higher loads than normal- and utility-category airplanes and therefore should be less apt to suffer overstress, the fact that it *is* an aerobatic airplane could cause some pilots to think it could take an unlimited amount of punishment. Some yahoo on a solo flight may decide to play fighter pilot in an airplane that can "take anything" and exceed the limit (flight) load factors. That same pilot might treat normal and utility category airplanes more gingerly.

While this preflight check is aimed at the 150/152 Aerobat, most of the points here can apply to other aerobatic airplanes. (The discussion of wing—and other—rivets doesn't apply to fabric-covered airplanes but you'd look for tears and wrinkles in the skin; also, you'd check the tailwheel instead of the nosewheel.)

3. Check the flap tracks for cracks, and the flap-actuating rod for freedom *and* security, as will be

shown by your instructor. Look for wrinkles and pulled rivets.

4. Check the left aileron for freedom of movement. As you move the aileron, check for slop between ailerons and see that the right aileron moves opposite to this one. (Airplanes *have* been misrigged!) Check the piano-wire hinges for security and be especially sure that the balance weight at the outboard leading edge of the aileron is secure. On any airplane, if a control balance-weight is lost, flutter could occur. The aileron-actuating rod may be rolled through a small arc. Look at the top of the whole wing for wrinkles and/or rivet problems.

5. Check the wing tip for security. Grasp the leading edge of the wing tip (but don't put stress on the plastic wing tip) and move it up and down briskly, checking for wrinkles or sounds of bending or cracking.

6. Move along the leading edge, checking it and the bottom surface of the wing.
   a. Look at the strut fairing, and check the pitot tube for obstruction. See that the fuel vent is clear and secure.
   b. Check the stall warner (the *Information Manual* suggests that it may be checked by a gentle suction through a clean handkerchief at the opening—don't use a dirty handkerchief).

7. a. Check the left tire and brake. Roll the airplane forward or backward by pulling on the wing strut to check the condition of the left main and nosewheel tire surfaces.
   b. Look for wrinkles or pulled rivets on the fuselage near the strut and landing gear junctions. (Hard landings could cause damage in this area.)
   c. See that the jettisonable-door hinge pins can freely move and that they are fully inserted.
   d. Make sure the static tube opening is clear.
   e. Note that the windshield is secure and has no cracks.
   f. Check that the wing root fairing has no screws missing.

8. a. Check the cowling fasteners for security.
   b. Check the nosewheel oleo for proper extension.
   c. Look at the tire again for wear or cuts and proper inflation.

9. a. Check the prop for nicks, and the spinner for security. (*Do not stand in the radius of the prop.*)
   b. Look inside the cowling for birds' nests and other foreign objects (rags, pliers, etc.). If you have to move the prop to do this, do it very carefully; assume that the magnetos are "hot." Check the alternator belt for wear (at least that part of it you can see).
   c. Stand back and check the carburetor air filter. Also look at the general symmetry of the airplane—is one wing lower than the other?
   d. Check the landing light for security and cracks.

10. a. Check this (the right) side of the cowling for security.
    b. See that the exhaust stack is firmly attached.
    c. Check the oil if you didn't do it in the initial fuel checks. Make sure that the oil dipstick and cover are secure.
    d. Check the right side of the windshield for cracks and security. The Aerobat will be dived to much faster speeds than the standard 150 or 152 normally encounters. The higher dynamic pressures could cause problems if there are a cracked windshield or semisecured fairings.

11. a. Check the right-side-door hinge pins for easy movement, then make sure that they are fully in.
    b. Make sure that the wing fairing is secure.
    c. Look for wrinkles or pulled rivets in the area of the junctures of landing gear and wing strut with fuselage.
    d. Check the right main tire for inflation and wear. (Roll the airplane.) Look at the brake and wheel assembly.

12. a. Look carefully at the leading edge and undersurface of the right wing.
    b. Check the area where the strut joins the wing for wrinkles or pulled rivets.

13. Shake the right wing as was done at step 5.

14. Look at the aileron hinge wires and balance weight.
    b. Check for slop in the aileron cable.
    c. Look at the top of the whole wing for wrinkles or pulled rivets.
    d. Make sure the aileron-actuating rod is secure but rollable through a small arc (see step 4).

15. Check the right flap and its tracks and actuating rod.

16. a. Examine the rear windows for security and cracks.
    b. Look at the side, top, and bottom of the fuselage for structural problems. Check any radio and ELT antennas in this general area for security.

17. a. Check the dorsal fin. Check the right horizontal stabilizer, both top and bottom, for possible damage from rocks or other debris thrown by the propeller.
    b. Look at the rudder stop and cable on this side.

18. a. Move the elevator to its full up and down limits and check the control stops for battering. See that the hinge bolt nuts are safetied. Push on the elevator *parallel* to its hinge line to check for any excess play.
    b. Check the elevator counterweight.
    c. Note the trim tab position to check it with the indicator in the cabin. Check the tab for excessive play. A rule of thumb is that the tab should not have more than $1/8$ in. play (compared with the elevator-tab hinge); more than this might call for a consultation with a mechanic. Check that the bolt on the tab-actuating rod is not worn and that the nut is safetied.

19. a. Move the rudder full travel each way, checking for bending and noting the condition of the rudder stops. Push on the rudder *parallel* to its hinge line to check for excess play.
  b. Look at the hinge bolts for wear and the safe-tying of nuts.
  c. Check the security of the rudder balance-weight, flashing beacon, and tail navigation light.
  d. Check that the rudder bendable trim tab is at a reasonable setting; if it's bent 90° to the rudder you should talk to someone knowledgeable about *why* it happens to be that way.
20. Examine the left elevator surfaces, movements, stops, hinges, and balance-weight (check step 18).
21. Give the left stabilizer a good check and look at the rudder cables and control stop.
22. Check the top, bottom, and left side of the fuselage in this area.

Okay, so you have checked the outside of the airplane thoroughly, and made sure the master and ignition switches were OFF before starting the check, but now there are other important points in the cabin you should know about. For instance, that anvil in the baggage compartment could cause problems. (*Nothing* should be in the baggage compartment during aerobatic maneuvers.) How about the ashtrays? You could be IFR in the cabin trying to peer through gum wrappers and other debris when you should be looking out at that reference point on the horizon.

As part of the preflight ritual of the first flight the instructor will see that your parachute fits properly and show you the best way to get into the airplane. There is no graceful way to get into the Aerobat with a chute on, so just be glad you made it.

You'll get the seat, shoulder harness, and belt adjusted so that you're secure in the airplane but can reach all controls properly. This is the point where you remember that the airplane ignition key is secure in your pants pocket under the flight suit and all that well-fastened parachute and seat belt/harness.

Once you're settled in, the instructor will review the procedure for exiting the airplane in flight. As the airline flight attendants' briefings say, this is an "unlikely event," but it's best to have the moves in mind before flying. The following steps are given for leaving the airplane:

1. Do *not* undo the belt and harness as a first step because if structural failure has occurred, forces may move and hold you in such a way that you cannot get out of the door.
2. Unlatch the door using the standard latch.
3. *Then* pull the emergency-door-release D ring.
4. Push the door clear of the airplane.
5. The left seat occupant (you) should grasp the forward doorpost with the right hand to help control your position after the belt/harness is released.
6. Release the belt/harness.

7. Roll out of the door opening head first, grabbing the landing gear step to pull you over the aft side of the landing gear.
8. Pull the ripcord (D-ring) after getting well clear of the airplane.

The instructor will be "assisting" you in getting out—the instructor can't leave until you do and so will be interested in expediting your departure.

A couple of more points:

When you are flying solo later, make sure the seat belt and shoulder harness of the other seat are secure.

Sometimes a pilot who is not used to wearing a parachute, after doing all the manipulation of buckles and straps, subconsciously feels all is secure. (In fact, that first time you get all suited up in the chute and seated in the airplane you'll feel *too* secure and wonder if you'll be able to move the controls at all. Don't worry, you'll very soon get used to it.) Anyway, on occasion aerobatic trainees have started to taxi out with seat belts and shoulder harnesses unattached to them. The instructor normally catches the problem right away but the solo trainee may not find out about it until that first inverted flight.

CHECKLIST FOR THE 1979 C-152 AEROBAT
Before Starting Engine
1. Preflight Inspection—COMPLETE.
2. Seats, Belts, Shoulder Harnesses—ADJUST and LOCK.
3. Fuel Shutoff Valve—ON.
4. Radios, Electrical Equipment—OFF.
5. Brakes—TEST and SET. (It's best not to depend on the parking brake in *any* airplane.)
6. Circuit Breakers—CHECK IN.

Starting Engine (temperatures above freezing)
1. Mixture—RICH.
2. Carburetor Heat—COLD.
3. Prime—AS REQUIRED (up to 3 strokes).
4. Throttle—OPEN ½ IN.
5. Propeller Area—CLEAR.
6. Master Switch—ON.
7. Ignition Switch—START (release when engine starts).
8. Throttle—ADJUST for 1000 rpm or less.
9. Oil Pressure—CHECK.

Before Takeoff
1. Parking Brake—SET. (Holding brakes is more reliable.)
2. Cabin Doors—CLOSED and LATCHED.
3. Flight Controls—FREE and CORRECT.
4. Flight Instruments—SET.

5. Fuel Shutoff Valve—ON.
6. Mixture—RICH (below 3000 ft).
7. Elevator Trim—TAKEOFF.
8. Throttle—1700 rpm.
   a. Magnetos—CHECK (rpm drop should not exceed 125 rpm on either magneto or 50 rpm differential between magnetos).
   b. Carburetor Heat—CHECK for rpm drop. Leave ON for 10 seconds to see if ice has been picked up during taxi and/or initial part of run-up.
   c. Engine Instruments and Ammeter—CHECK.
   d. Suction Gage—CHECK.
9. Radios—SET.
10. Flashing Beacon, Navigation Lights and/or Strobe Lights— ON as required.
11. Throttle Friction Lock—ADJUST.
12. Brakes—RELEASE.

Takeoff
NORMAL TAKEOFF
1. Wing flaps—0°–10°.
2. Carburetor Heat—COLD.
3. Throttle—FULL OPEN.
4. Elevator Control—LIFT NOSEWHEEL at 50 KIAS.
5. Climb Speed—65–75 KIAS.

SHORT-FIELD TAKEOFF
1. Wing Flaps—10°
2. Carburetor Heat—COLD.
3. Brakes—APPLY.
4. Throttle—FULL OPEN.
5. Mixture—RICH below 3000 ft, then LEAN to obtain maximum rpm.
6. Brakes—RELEASE.
7. Elevator Control—SLIGHTLY TAIL LOW.
8. Climb Speed—54 KIAS (until all obstacles are cleared).
9. Wing Flaps—RETRACT slowly after reaching 60 KIAS.

Enroute Climb
1. Airspeed—70–80 KIAS. (Max rate of climb speed at max weight at sea level is 67 K. Decrease KIAS by about ½ K/1000 ft density altitude.)
2. Throttle—FULL OPEN.

3. Mixture—RICH below 3000 ft, then LEAN for maximum rpm.

Cruise
1. Power—1900–2550 rpm (no more than 75%).
2. Elevator Trim—ADJUST.
3. Mixture—LEAN.

Before Landing
1. Seats, Belts, Harnesses—ADJUST and LOCK.
2. Mixture—RICH.
3. Carburetor Heat—ON (apply full heat before closing throttle).

Landing
NORMAL LANDING
1. Airspeed—60–70 KIAS (flaps UP).
2. Wing Flaps—AS DESIRED (below 85 KIAS).
3. Airspeed—55–65 KIAS (flaps DOWN).
4. Touchdown—MAIN WHEELS FIRST.
5. Landing Roll—LOWER NOSEWHEEL GENTLY.
6. Braking—MINIMUM REQUIRED.

BALKED LANDING
1. Throttle—FULL OPEN.
2. Carburetor Heat—COLD.
3. Wing Flaps—RETRACT TO 20°.
4. Airspeed—55 KIAS.
5. Wing Flaps—RETRACT (slowly).

After Landing
1. Wing Flaps—UP.
2. Carburetor Heat—COLD.

Securing Airplane
1. Parking Brake—SET. (Chocks, or better yet, tiedowns, are more dependable.)
2. Radios, Electrical Equipment—OFF.
3. Mixture—IDLE CUTOFF (pull full out).
4. Ignition Switch—OFF.
5. Master Switch—OFF.
6. Control Lock—INSTALL.

Keep a sharp lookout for other airplanes because you won't be doing much straight and level flying on this first flight (and others to follow).

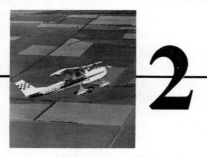

2

PREPARATORY MANEUVERS

THE MANEUVERS in this chapter are intended to give you a good feel for the airplane in preparation for the basic aerobatic maneuvers. You may want to start learning aileron rolls and more exotic maneuvers, but it's to your advantage to have a good feel of the airplane at various speeds and attitudes before proceeding with basic aerobatics. Here you'll establish habit patterns for safe aerobatic flying (or any flying, for that matter).

Always clear the area before starting a maneuver or sequence of maneuvers. The airplane will be rapidly changing attitudes, altitudes, and headings, and as mentioned earlier, coming out of a loop or other maneuver and finding yourself face-to-face with another airplane is a disappointing situation, indeed.

A fact of life of airplane performance is that *control effectiveness* is a combination of *deflection and calibrated airspeed* (*control effectiveness = deflection × CAS*). While true for all types of flying, this is even more important in aerobatics, where airspeed values may vary widely in one maneuver (the loop and its variations come immediately to mind). A milder example is the aileron roll, which has an entry speed in the Aerobat of 115 K and a completion speed of about 80 K; as the airspeed decays, the rudder (and ailerons and elevator) need to be deflected more to get the same effect. (More about this, later.)

The airplane reacts the same to control inputs, *as far as you are concerned,* whether the airplane is inverted or upright. (A specific note will be brought up in the introduction to the loop, in Chap. 4.) If you ease back on the control wheel, the nose will "move toward you"; moving the wheel forward will ease the nose "away from you." The same applies to yaw and roll, *but* later, when you are competing or doing airshows, you'll have to take into account what you'll do to get a specific path with relation to the ground.

For purposes of easy remembering, a power setting of 2300 rpm (C-152 Aerobat) and 2500 rpm (C-150 Aerobat) will be used as "normal cruise" for all maneuvers in this manual, unless otherwise stated. Keep in mind that the general principles cited in this manual apply to basic aerobatic instruction regardless of particular airplane entry speeds or power settings.

STALLS

1-g STALLS

After getting to a safe altitude the instructor may have you review some of the stalls you practiced for the private (or other) certificate some time ago. The point is that you'll want to get the feel and get used again to the idea of deliberately stalling an airplane. You'll be hearing the stall warner quite often during the performance of some of the maneuvers, and it's better to be comfortable with stalls and have quick and effective recovery available if one of the maneuvers goes awry. You'll be high enough for safety during any of the maneuvers, but a poorly recovered inadvertent stall can cost extra altitude, which can take time to get back on a hot summer day. Also, this practice can be a confidence builder; there are plenty of private and commercial pilots who have never felt comfortable with plain, old-fashioned power-on *or* power-off stalls and are secretly nervous about them. In fact, they worry more about stalls in an aerobatic course than doing a loop or roll. There will be inadvertent stalls occurring during the course, as well as deliberate snap rolls (accelerated stalls) and spins.

Common Errors in 1-g Stalls

1. Failing to clear the area before doing straight-ahead stalls.

2. Pulling the nose too high in the power-off stall.

3. Not allowing a stall break—recovering at the first indication of buffeting.

4. Using poor recovery techniques—not relaxing enough back pressure during the recovery, resulting in buffeting and wallowing of the airplane continuing, or overenthusiastic pushing forward of the control wheel so that excess altitude is lost.

ACCELERATED STALLS

You know that a stall is caused by a too-great angle of attack—not by slow airspeed. The airplane can be stalled at any airspeed and attitude (disregarding stress problems), and you may find later that by using excessive back pressure on the back side of a loop you can feel the stall nibble—or break—even though the nose is pointed straight down. One possible problem with *accelerated stalls* (the term means that above-normal acceleration forces are in action when the airplane stalls) is that they can be done at too high a speed, and you'll find that the maneuvering speed is the limiting factor for abrupt, full deflection of the controls. At lower weights, the maneuvering speed, which is 108 K (120 mph) for the Aerobat (at the maximum certificated weight), is decreased, so to be well on the safe side, any deliberate accelerated stall maneuvers (such as the snap roll) should be performed at a *maximum* airspeed of 90 K (80 K is the recommended entry speed for snap rolls).

The acceleration forces imposed on the airplane in a stall are a function of the square of the speed at which stall may be recognized if encountered in "normal" flying.

PROCEDURE IN ACCELERATED STALLS. First, look at the accelerated stall as an introduction to snap maneuvers. Clear the area and establish a 45° bank at a power setting of 2300 rpm (2500 rpm). Slow the airplane to 80 K (90 mph) by gradually increasing back pressure. As the airspeed settles on 80 K (90 mph), smoothly but quickly move the control wheel straight back to the full-aft position so that the airplane is stalled at a higher-than-normal airspeed. (Don't use aileron or rudder during the stall entry.) Recover by relaxing back pressure or applying positive forward pressure, as in the procedure for any stalled condition, and adding more power (if available) to decrease altitude loss.

Practice this type of accelerated stall from turns in both directions. Again, don't use any aileron or rudder during the initiation or recovery. One reason for the 45° bank is that most pilots get into an accelerated stall when they try to *"tighten the turn."* Their actions may not be as deliberately rapid as yours, but they can usually get the same result, and unfortunately, they may be trying to tighten that final turn on approach. Another reason is that if the pull-up is made wings-level the nose could be raised straight up, creating the possibility of a whip stall, or tail slide. The banked attitude ensures that a whip stall is avoided.

Another method of setting up an accelerated stall situation is to establish a bank of 45° or more and increase the angle of attack at a constant altitude or in a moderate rate of climb until the stall occurs. Power may be reduced below cruising, but any decrease in the rate of climb or a loss of altitude might spoil the effect by relieving the load factor (hence, no accelerated stall). You can figure on the stall occurring at about 20 percent higher airspeed than "normal" in a 45° bank and about 40 percent higher in a 60° bank. It has been suggested that accelerated stalls done in other than aerobatic airplanes should not be started at a speed higher than 1.25 times the normal stall speed. Since the Aerobat is certificated in the aerobatic category, stalling it at up to 1.60 times the normal calibrated stall speed at max weight is an allowed and safe operation. On a flight test you won't be using flaps while demonstrating accelerated stalls. And while the subject is being discussed, you won't do *any* aerobatic maneuvers (including spins) with the flaps extended.

On a flight test you are to avoid such problems during the recovery as a secondary stall, an inadvertent spin, exceeding the airspeed limitations of the airplane, or moving the examiner's voice up a couple of octaves. (This type of flying is what might be expected of pilots who are not trained in aerobatics.)

By experiencing both types of accelerated stalls you can see different situations where a stall could occur in normal operations.

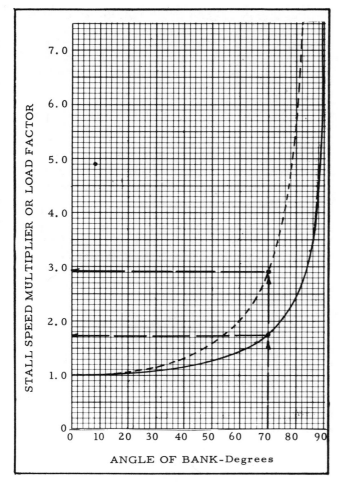

Fig. 2-1. Stall speed multiplier (*solid line*) and load factor (*dashed line*) versus angle of bank in a constant-altitude turn. At 70° of bank, the load factor is 2.92 g and the stall speed is increased by a factor of approximately 1.71. An airplane that stalls at 60 K at 1 g would stall at 1.71 × 60 = 103 K.

To find the stall speed multiplier for turns *and* pull-ups, take the square root of the load factor (a calculator with this function is useful).

it is stalled (Fig. 2-1); that is, when you slow the airplane gradually and stall it at the normal stall speed, 1 g results and it's not an accelerated stall. If you use the elevators in such a manner that the airplane is stalled at *twice* the normal stall airspeed, 4 g's will result ($2^2 = 4$, obviously). If you were so unthinking as to stall an airplane at *3* times the normal stall speed, 9 g's would result (as well as a number of bent or broken parts, depending on the certification category).

There are three main reasons for the practice of accelerated stalls here: (1) as an introduction to the snap roll and inadvertent accelerated stalls during various aerobatic maneuvers, (2) to become familiar with this maneuver for a flight test, and (3) so that this type of

Common Errors in the Accelerated Stall

1. Moving the control wheel back too slowly so that the stall is not accelerated.

2. Not maintaining the 45° bank—allowing it to shallow.

3. Allowing the nose to drop just before the stall is induced so that the airspeed increases to above the safe value for inducing the stall (the procedure must be started again).

4. Making a too-abrupt recovery, with movement toward zero g or even negative g.

STEEP POWER TURNS

This is a good maneuver for getting back to feeling comfortable in steeper banks when you've been doing mostly straight and level flying. It will help you get the feel of the airplane, as well as smoothing your coordination and improving your planning ability.

The steep power turn, as such, is a required maneuver on the private and commercial flight tests.

The desired angle of bank of the steep power turn for the private flight test is 40–50° (called a *constant-altitude turn* there) and for the commercial flight test is 50 ± 5°. Limits on the commercial are ± 100 ft of the entry altitude and ± 10° from the entry heading. For introduction to an aerobatic course, an average of 60° of bank and 720° of turn is suggested (Fig. 2-2).

PROCEDURE IN STEEP POWER TURNS. At a safe altitude and clear area, pick a prominent landmark on the horizon to use as a reference.

Clear the area and roll smoothly into the desired angle of bank. As the roll-in is made, smoothly open the throttle as necessary to help maintain altitude throughout the turn.

One of the problems you might have is anticipating the back pressure to be required in this steeper bank and adding too much, too soon, as you roll in. This, coupled with an overly hasty power increase, could result in an altitude gain at the beginning of the maneuver, setting up a problem that could persist throughout the rest of the turn.

If you are gaining altitude after the turn is established, steepen the bank slightly and relax some of the back pressure. Since the bank will be 60° and the altitude constant (it says here), the accelerometer will be right at +2 g's.

If you are losing altitude, shallow the bank slightly before increasing back pressure. Increasing the back pressure without shallowing the bank puts higher load factors on the airplane and is little or no help in stopping the altitude loss. (The chances are that the altitude loss rate will be *increased* sharply by tightening the turn without shallowing the bank.)

If it becomes evident that things aren't going the way you planned—and may be getting worse—it's best

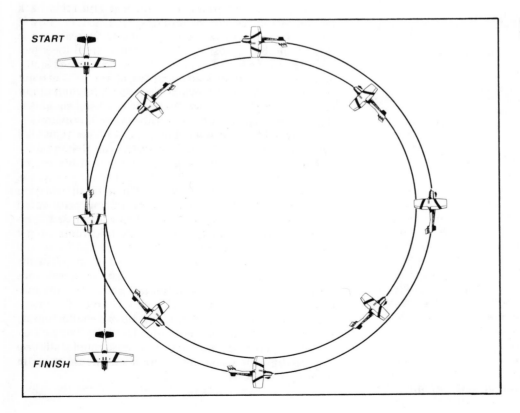

Fig. 2-2. The 720° steep power turn.

START

FINISH

to stop immediately. For instance, if you lose 500 ft in the first 360° of turn and things are generally turning into a Chinese fire drill, why not recover and try it again?

Check your bank, nose position, and altimeter as you turn. Get onto any deviations right away, because they usually indicate a trend that could give trouble in a short while.

Remember the *"torque"* (left-turning effects); since you will be indicating slower than cruise and using higher power, right rudder may be needed to keep the ball centered, particularly in a right turn.

Keep up with the reference point; a 1080° turn or making an extra circle doesn't show your planning ability in its best light.

Some pilots want to use the heading indicator as a roll-out reference, but it's best to use an outside reference for heading. Besides, at the 60° bank the heading indicator may "slip" and become inaccurate. You don't want to have your head down in the cockpit while making such a fast direction change—you might meet another airplane.

One problem you may have is the nose rising on the roll-out. It takes conscious effort to keep it down as the wings are leveled. The problem is greater if you don't ease the throttle back to cruise as the roll-out is started.

One good procedure is to roll from one 720° power turn into one in the opposite direction; this will iron out any problems in altitude control (or indicate what your problems are). You can roll into the opposite turn *without* changing power, or you can practice changing power during the transition to the new turn.

One problem that pilots have in doing steep turns (or any turns for that matter) in a side-by-side airplane such as the Aerobat is failing to realize that the nose position *appears* to be different for left and right turns.

When you are sitting on the left (the pilot's) side, the nose appears high in a left turn and low in a right turn. Actually *a point on the cowling directly in front of you* would be at the same position in a left *or* right steep turn (Fig. 2-3).

Common Errors in Steep Power Turns

1. Applying too much back pressure at the beginning of the roll-in—the airplane gains altitude.

2. Applying power roughly or too rapidly at the beginning of the roll-in—possibly causing engine overspeed.

3. Using back pressure alone in attempting to correct for a nose-low condition, forgetting that the bank must be shallowed.

4. Using the center of the cowling for pitch reference, instead of a point directly in front of the pilot.

5. "Losing" the reference point.

6. Forgetting "torque" correction or having other coordination problems.

7. Letting the nose rise on roll-out—usually a re-

Fig. 2-3. View from the left seat in left and right 60°-banked turns. A point on the cowling should be at the same relative position to the horizon when turning in either direction.

sult of neglecting to retard the throttle and relax back pressure as the wings are leveled.

THE CHANDELLE

The chandelle is a required maneuver for the commercial certificate and is also good introduction to maneuvers that require simultaneous altitude and airspeed changes and turns to predetermined headings.

The chandelle is a maximum performance climbing turn with a 180° change in direction (Figs. 2-4 and 2-5). The airspeed will vary from slightly above cruise to just above a stall.

Good planning is required, and since the speed is changing from the Aerobat recommended entry speed of 105 K (120 mph) to just above a stall, your coordination must take care of changing control pressures and "torque" effects. It's best to make the initial bank and turn into the wind, so that you don't get too far away from the starting point. (The wind, however, has nothing to do with the actual performance of the maneuver—as you know.)

A straight stretch of road or railroad makes a good reference, and you may start the chandelle flying either parallel or perpendicular to it. For most people, starting the dive perpendicular to the reference makes for better checking of the 90° point of turn.

A reference point on the horizon (into the wind)

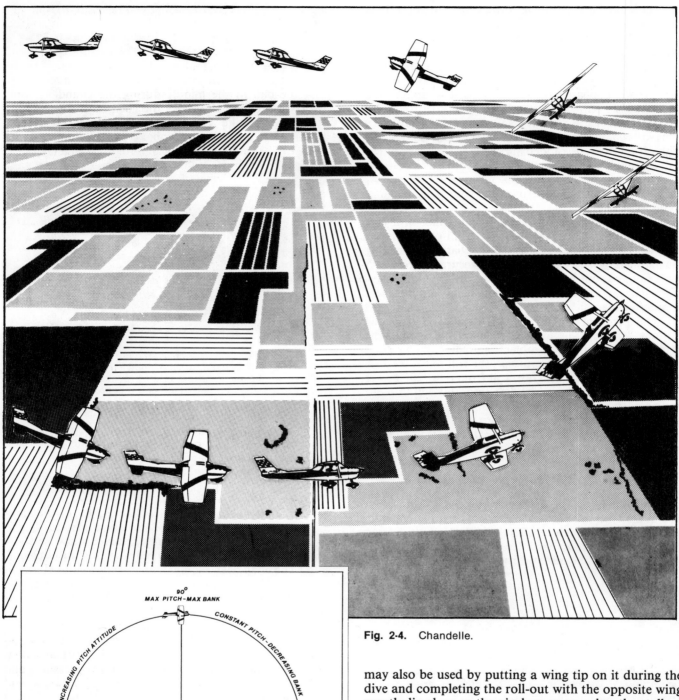

Fig. 2-4. Chandelle.

may also be used by putting a wing tip on it during the dive and completing the roll-out with the opposite wing exactly lined up as the airplane approaches the stall.

One big problem for pilots in doing chandelles at first is not looking outside and keeping up with the reference. This often results in either a too-early roll-out or a last-minute accelerated roll-out as the pilot suddenly realizes the airplane is about to turn more than 180°.

PROCEDURE IN THE CHANDELLE. Fig. 2-6A–H shows the chandelle in sequence.

90°
MAX PITCH–MAX BANK

INCREASING PITCH ATTITUDE

CONSTANT PITCH – DECREASING BANK

ENTRY SPEED
INITIAL BANK

WINGS LEVEL
JUST ABOVE STALL

CHANDELLE

Fig. 2-5. Elements of the chandelle.

Line up parallel with, or perpendicular to, a road, railroad, or section line (Fig. 2-6A).

Ease the Aerobat nose over to pick up 105 K (120 mph), making sure that the rpm red line is not exceeded (Fig. 2-6B). Some airplanes must be *slowed* below the maneuvering speed when starting a chandelle.

As you approach 105 K, bank the airplane 30° with coordinated controls (Fig. 2-6C). Because of the bank, the airplane will turn slightly before the pull-up is started—which is the way it should be. *Don't* hold opposite rudder to stop the turn. Keep the ball centered throughout the maneuver. (Neutralize the ailerons so that no further roll is induced as the nose is raised to the climb attitude.) The apparent bank will increase to about 45° as the nose reaches the 90° position, but this is because of the attitude of the airplane, *not* because of any added roll induced by the ailerons. Your instructor, however, may require a constant bank from the initial bank to the 90°-turn position. This means that you will be using opposite aileron (and rudder) as necessary to maintain a constant 30° until the roll-out starts.

Apply power smoothly as the nose is raised to the climb position (Fig. 2-6D). Be prepared to correct for "torque." To keep a smooth operation, open the throttle as the airspeed drops to attempt to maintain the cruise rpm. (Full power is applied in the Aerobat. Other airplanes, with constant-speed propellers, may maintain a fixed power setting throughout the chandelle. The *Pilot's Operating Handbook* and/or your instructor will give the procedure.)

The nose is in the process of being raised *only* in the first 90° of turn. At the 90° point of turn, the maximum pitch attitude is reached and maintained (Fig. 2-6E). (This is also the steepest bank, if you weren't trying to hold a constant bank of 30°.) Gradually roll out the airplane (Fig. 2-6F), so that at 180° of turn the wings are level and the airspeed is just above a stall (Fig. 2-6G) (don't raise the nose any higher after the 90° point—continue a constant pitch and constant rate of roll-out for the last 90° of turn). Maintain this condition for 10–20 seconds to prove it wasn't just luck that got the airplane to this point. Then lower the nose to return to normal cruise at the 180° position (Fig. 2-6H).

A quick howgozit for the Aerobat is an airspeed of 70 K (80 mph) as the nose moves through the 90° point of turn. Faster than this and you won't be close to the stall (the nose will be too low) as the roll-out is completed. Slower than this and the nose may have to be lowered during the last 90° of turn to avoid a stall. This may seem like a mechanical crutch but can help in working out pitch problems during the last 90° of turn. Naturally, other airplanes will have different entry (and 90°-point) airspeeds, and after a couple of chandelles you can get some numbers for them (a *quick* glance at the airspeed is sufficient).

Watch that correction for "torque." If insufficient right rudder is held in a chandelle to the right, the usual result is that the turn slows down and may be stopped before reaching 180° of turn (and there you are—30°

short). In a chandelle to the left, neglect of the left-turning tendency usually results in the airplane turning to the 180° point too soon so the pilot has to make a rapid roll-out. The ideal roll-out procedure is a coordinated one at a constant rate from the 90° point to the 180° position. Some pilots aren't concerned about keeping the ball in the middle during the chandelle, only worrying if the ball breaks the glass and leaves the instrument—unlike you, they're the "stunt pilot" type rather than a precision aerobatic pilot.

If you gain a couple of hundred feet in a chandelle in the Aerobat (and have had good coordination and planning), consider it a success. The point is to develop your technique so that when you fly that F-16 later, you'll gain *several thousand feet* per chandelle.

During the first couple of chandelles you'll likely feel like you have two left feet, but you'll soon get the idea.

Common Errors in the Chandelle

1. Making initial bank too shallow, so that as the nose continues to be eased up, the airspeed is too low for the amount of turn—a stall is possible before the turn is completed.

2. Making a too-steep initial bank—a maneuver that is all turn with little altitude gain.

3. Having coordination problems on the initial bank—the usual tendency is not to use enough rudder.

4. Not neutralizing the ailerons—making the bank too steep at the 90° position.

5. Having power problems—forgetting to open the throttle or opening it too soon.

6. Not using "torque" correction, particularly during the last 90° of turn.

7. Not looking at the reference (road, railroad, or section line)—instead staring over the nose.

8. Starting the roll-out too late or starting well after passing the 90° point.

9. Keeping the nose too low all the way around so that the airspeed is not near the stall at the 180° point.

10. Becoming so engrossed in airspeed and altitude that the 180° reference point is neglected or lost—completing the roll-out too soon or too late.

THE WINGOVER

The wingover is a good exercise in coordination and also serves as an introduction to the lazy eight, a required maneuver on the commercial flight test. The wingover is basically a 90° climbing turn followed by a 90° diving turn in the same direction with a 180° change in direction. (The lazy eight is discussed in the following section.)

The maximum angle of bank in the wingover is found at the 90° position, but the bank will be 60° when the maneuver is first practiced. Later, the bank may be vertical at the steepest point.

The maneuver is coordinated, and the ball should be centered throughout. This requires judicious use of

Fig. 2-6A-H. Chandelle as seen from the cockpit and from outside the airplane.

(A) Lining up with the reference line.

(B) Easing the nose over to establish the recommended entry speed.

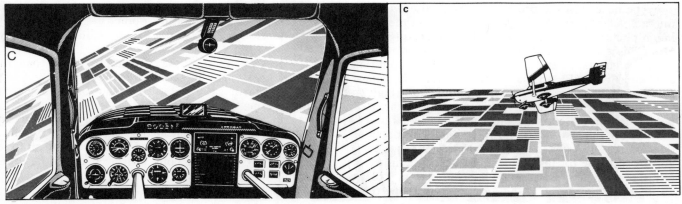

(C) Bank of 30° in the desired direction of turn (to the right here).

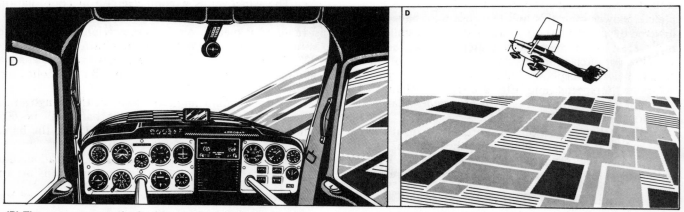

(D) The nose crosses the horizon, and power is applied.

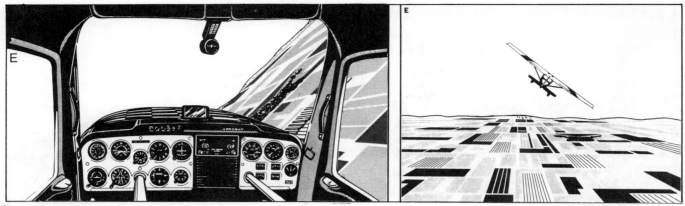

(E) The 90°-turn position and the maximum pitch attitude.

(F) The 135°-turn position (pitch constant, roll-out continuing, airspeed decreasing).

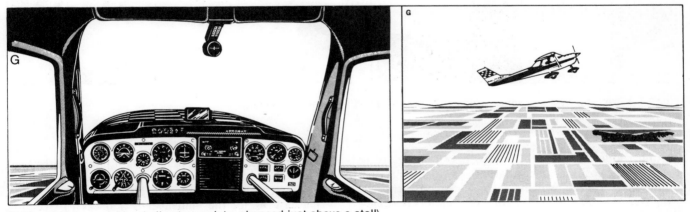

(G) The 180°-turn position (roll-out complete, airspeed just above a stall).

(H) Level cruising airspeed and power setting resumed.

19

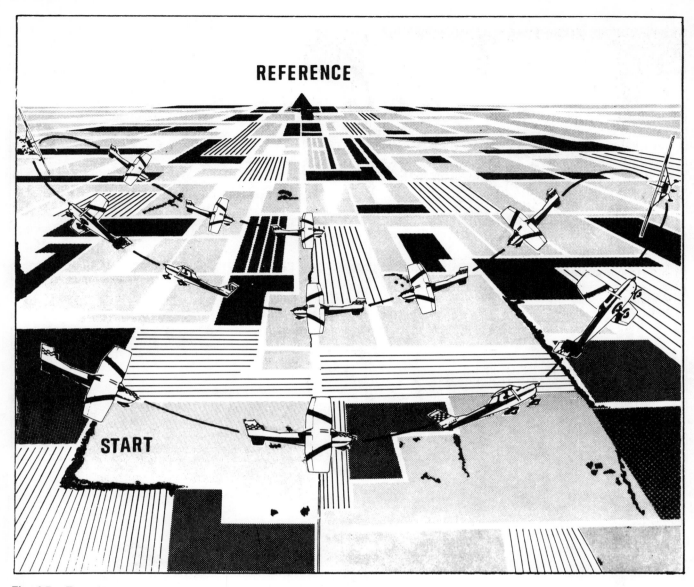

Fig. 2-7. Two wingovers in a series. This might be considered a steeper lazy eight.

bottom rudder (and maybe some opposite aileron) at the 90°-turn position, particularly in a wingover to the right, since "torque" will be a factor to consider. The wingover is a good maneuver for maintaining coordination throughout constantly changing banks and airspeeds. Fig. 2-7 shows two wingovers in a series, with 60° maximum banks (constant power).

PROCEDURE IN THE WINGOVER. Pick an easy-to-see reference on the horizon (preferably into the wind if you plan a series of wingovers). Clear the area as you turn to put it exactly under the wing tip, 90° to the longitudinal axis. (The row of rivets on the Aerobat that run out the wing are a useful reference—your instructor will show you.)

Lower the nose (wings level) to pick up an airspeed of 105 K (120 mph); before the dive set the throttle at the 2300-rpm (2500-rpm) cruise value as recommended and don't change it during the wingover. Ease the nose up, and as it reaches the level attitude, start a coordinated climbing turn, for example, to the left. At 45° of

turn the nose should be at its highest pitch and the bank at 30°, one-half the maximum bank. The steepest bank and lowest airspeed should be at the 90°-turn position. The last 90° of the maneuver is a smooth descending turn. The airplane should be headed exactly 180° from its original heading, and the airspeed should be at 105 K (120 mph) when the wingover is completed (it says here). The altitude should be that at the beginning of the initial pull-up.

Your line of sight should pass through the reference at the steepest point of bank (and lowest airspeed) just as the diving turn part (the last 90°) of the maneuver begins. The wingover is complete when the opposite wing tip is pointing at the reference point. Again, the highest pitch attitude of the nose, and half the maximum bank, should be at 45° of turn, the *lowest* pitch and half the maximum bank will be found at 135° of turn.

Note the altitude of initial pull-up at 105 K. If you have the power set up properly and fly a good wingover, you should complete the 180° of turn and bottom out at

105 K and that same altitude. It's a good feeling to be doing lazy eights, or a series of wingovers, and see that you're coming out right on the airspeed and altitude each time.

As will be noted later, the wingover is a good (if somewhat mild) introduction to the barrel roll, which some pilots consider a wingover carried to the ultimate. If you have a handle on the wingover, particularly with a vertical bank, you'll have a good start on the barrel roll.

The wingover is a good way to reverse course with a small turn radius, since the low airspeed at the peak of the maneuver allows a quick turn. A variation of the technique is to start the maneuver from normal cruising flight. However, some faster airplanes are required to slow down below the max weight maneuvering speed before starting the maneuver as was noted for the chandelle. Wingovers may be done in a series, reversing the direction of turn after each one, as shown in Fig. 2-7.

Common Errors in the Wingover

1. Starting the turn too soon, before the nose crosses the level flight attitude.

2. Using too steep an initial bank or too much roll for the pull-up—this results in much turn and little climb, with a too-high airspeed at the 90° point.

3. Slipping at the 90°-turn point, particularly in the wingover to the right.

4. "Losing" the reference point so that the turn is not exactly 180°.

5. Ending the maneuver off-altitude and off-airspeed (the commonest error of all).

6. Rolling out too soon, not completing the full 180° of turn (this is more of a problem with shallow-banked wingovers and the 30°-maximum-bank lazy eight).

THE LAZY EIGHT

The lazy eight, a required maneuver on the commercial flight test, may be considered at first as a series of *shallow* (30°-maximum-bank) left and right wingovers with no hesitation between them. With practice you'll see it as one maneuver, with no transition from one part to the other (Fig. 2-8).

It's called the *lazy eight* because an extension of the

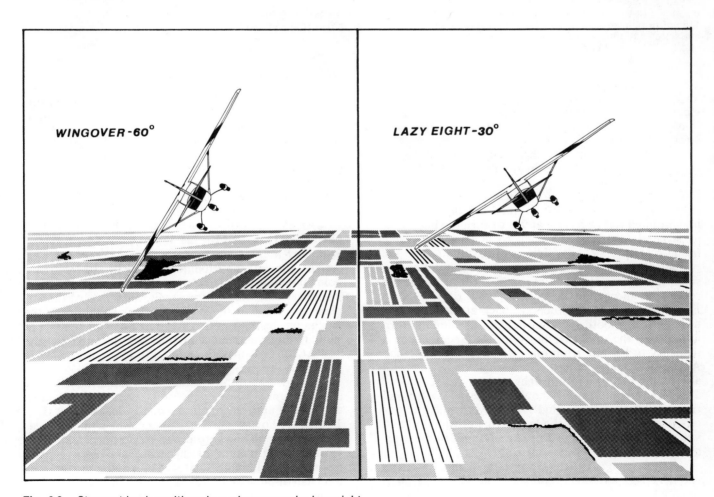

Fig. 2.8. Steepest bank positions in a wingover and a lazy eight.

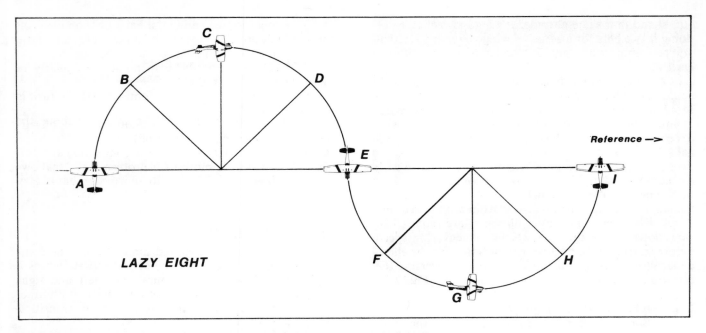

Fig. 2-9. Top view of a lazy eight (constant power): Beginning of maneuver, reference point picked (point *A*); at 45° of turn, airplane at highest pitch and one-half of maximum bank (point *B*); at 90° of turn, longitudinal axis level, maximum 30° bank, slowest airspeed (point *C*); at 135° of turn, lowest pitch, one-half of maximum bank (point *D*); at 180° of turn, wings level, initial pull-up altitude and airspeed (point *E*), Points *F, G, H,* and *I* are comparable to *B, C, D,* and *E* in pitch and bank attitudes and airspeeds.

airplane's longitudinal axis transcribes a large figure eight lying on its side on the horizon. From above, the maneuver is seen as S-turns across an imaginary straight line (Fig. 2-9, points *A–I*).

After a wing tip reference point is picked (point *A*), the nose is eased over to the recommended entry speed and a smooth pull-up is started. As the nose crosses the horizon, a shallow climbing turn is initiated. Like the wingover, at 45° of turn the nose is at its highest pitch (point *B*) and at 90° of turn the bank is at its steepest (30°) and the airspeed at its lowest value (point *C*). At the 90° position an extension of your line of sight should pass through the reference point as you smoothly fly the airplane into a diving turn, gradually rolling out and pulling up so that at 180° of turn (point *E*) the airspeed and altitude are back at the entry values. Then a smooth (without hesitation) climbing turn is made in the opposite direction. At first there is a tendency to hesitate from one "wingover" to the other. Again, it should be considered a single maneuver with alternating phases left and right.

The reference point should be picked so that all turns will be made upwind. It's easy to make a fair cross-country by doing the lazy eights downwind, and you may find that you've drifted well out of the practice area when the series is complete.

The lazy eight is strictly a training maneuver and is excellent for developing coordination and good planning habits.

PROCEDURE IN THE LAZY EIGHT. Put the selected horizon reference point (preferably into the wind) directly off a wing (Fig. 2-10A), set the power to 2300 rpm (2500 rpm), at about 85 K cruise and ease the nose over to a shallow dive. As 105 K (120 mph) is reached, ease the nose up into a shallow climb and as the nose crosses the horizon, start a coordinated turn toward the reference. Check the ball for possible slipping or skidding problems, but don't stare at it.

At 45° of turn the airplane will be at its highest pitch and at one-half the maximum bank (15° in Fig. 2-9, point *B*).

At the 90° position (Fig. 2-10C), the reference point should appear to be moving smoothly through an imaginary extension of the longitudinal axis of the airplane (your line of sight) and the bank should be at the maximum bank of 30°. At this point the airspeed should be just above a stall and the ball centered.

At 135° of turn, the pitch attitude is at the lowest point and the bank is one-half the maximum.

As the extension of the longitudinal axis of the airplane moves through the point, continue a shallow diving turn until the opposite wing is on the point (Fig. 2-10E). Without hesitation, ease the nose up into a shallow climbing turn toward the reference. Repeat the previous moves (longitudinal axis through the point, followed by a shallow diving turn). Continue the series as long as you desire.

The patterns should be symmetrical; that is, the

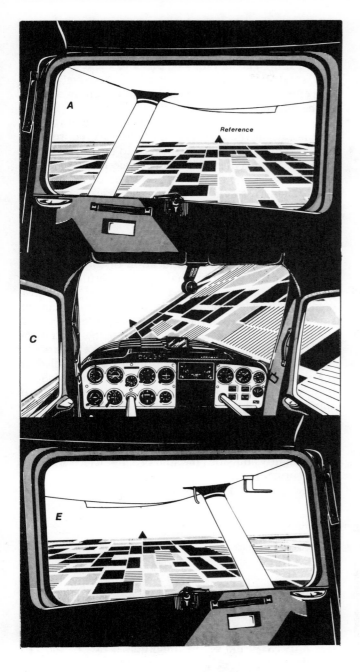

same altitude at the "bottom" of each 180° turn, as for the wingover series.

Common Errors in the Lazy Eight

1. Allowing too steep a bank at the peak of the maneuver (you'll find that it's pretty tough to hold it down to 30°).

2. Using too-abrupt back pressure—pulling the nose too high and stalling before, or at, reaching the 90° point.

3. Using poor coordination—slipping or skidding.

4. Gaining altitude for the shallow bank of 30° (the usual tendency in the maneuver after being used to the steeper banks, and greater back pressure, of the wingover).

One last note on the lazy eight: Sometimes an extended series of this maneuver can lead to Not So Much Fun Anymore (see the section on physical condition in Chap. 1). Let the instructor know if NSMFA is occurring, so you can take a break or move on to other maneuvers.

Fig. 2-10. Part of a lazy eight as seen from the cockpit. Views **A, C,** and **E** are seen at those same points in Fig. 2-9.

nose should move above or below the horizon an equal amount. Any persistent gain or loss of altitude is disqualifying on the commercial flight test. You may have to vary the initial power setting slightly to correct for large variations in airplane weight or major density altitude changes. In other words, if you are losing altitude in the series, increase the power; if gaining altitude, reduce the power. Try to have 105 K (120 mph) and the

3
SPINS

A GENERAL REVIEW OF SPIRALS AND SPINS

Many pilots are not aware of the difference between a spiral and a spin and often think in terms of one when the other one is the problem. Fig. 3-1 shows a comparison of instrument indications for the two flight conditions.

A *spiral* is a steep, diving turn with a low angle of attack and high (usually increasing) airspeed. The average 2-hour student should be able to recover easily from a spiral because the controls are used normally; the wings are leveled with *coordinated* aileron and rudder *pressures* and the nose brought up by back *pressure*. The situation is an exaggerated version of the already familiar descending turn.

A *spin* may look like a spiral to pilots with little or no experience with spins, but the controls aren't acting like it, even though they keep trying a spiral recovery. Pilots have to think of *mechanical control movements* rather than pressure for spin recovery. They have to move the elevators in a direction that, by the looks of it, will make things worse.

Looking at Fig. 3-1A, you can see that the spiral has a high airspeed and the small airplane in the turn coordinator is well deflected but probably not as much as in a spin. The ball may be offset to the left for most U.S. single-engine airplanes because of "torque" correction effects. (The ball tends to be to the right in a climb, to the left in higher-speed dives.)

The spin (Fig. 3-1B) shows a higher rate of rotation (the needle in the turn and slip, the turn coordinator airplane, and both balls are pegged to the left). In some cases the ball may be oscillating betweeen the center and full-left deflection. You may have heard that the ball goes outside the spin so you should "kick the ball" to start the recovery. *Don't*—the ball is not a reliable indicator of spin direction.

The ball in the turn and slip or turn coordinator should *not* be used to check for spin direction, because its reaction depends on the location of this instrument on the panel, or more technically, its position with respect to the airplane's center of gravity. If the instrument is on the left (pilot's) side, as it is in most current side-by-side airplanes, the ball will be on the left side of the race in both right and left spins for the Cessna 150 and 152 Aerobat, Cherokee 140B, Musketeer Aerobatic Sport III, and Tomahawk. Slip indicators installed on the right side of the panels in the Aerobat and Sport had the ball going to the right side of the instrument in spins in both directions (Fig. 3-2). So don't "kick the ball" if you are in a spin. You have a 50 percent chance of being correct in the installation just mentioned. A ball in the middle of the instrument panel *may* react to move slightly "outside" the spin or may sit in the middle of the instrument.

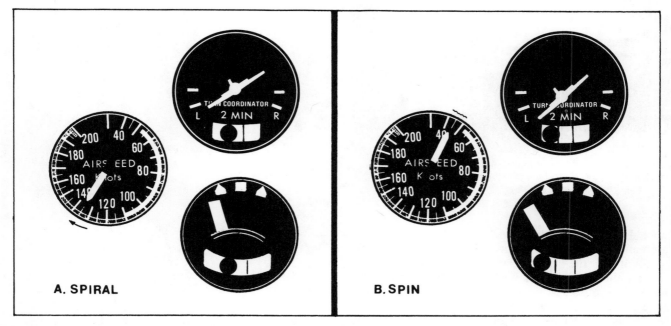

Fig. 3-1. Instrument indications in a spiral and spin. The instruments shown are on the pilot's (left) side of the panel. (From *The Flight Instructor's Manual*)

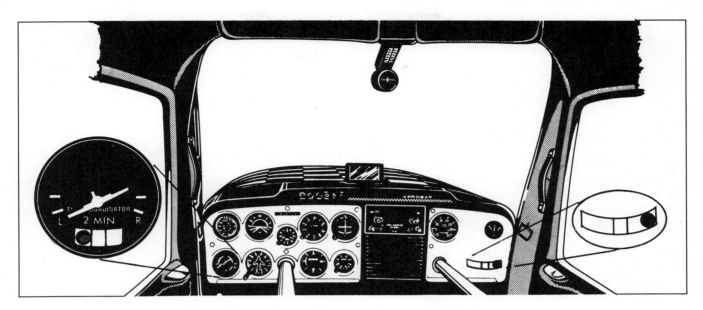

Fig. 3-2. Indications of a turn coordinator (left, or pilot's, side) and a slip indicator (right side) in a developed spin in an Aerobat.

A snap roll is defined as a horizontal spin resulting from accelerated use of rudder and elevator. It is like a speeded-up movie of a pilot using the controls for a spin entry. (Chap. 4 covers the snap roll in detail.)

In the snap roll, because of the higher g forces and (usually) faster rate of roll, it would seem that the ball would always end up on the "outside" of the maneuver. *Not so,* as you can see by the snap roll turn and slip indications in Fig. 3-3.

To recover by reference to instruments (partial panel), apply rudder *opposite* to the needle (turn and slip) or small airplane's indication of turn (turn coor-

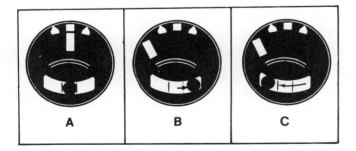

Fig. 3-3. Turn and slip indications on the left (pilot's) side in a Musketeer Aerobatic Sport III (N6544T) during a snap roll. **(A)** The airplane is at the attitude and airspeed to start the snap roll but no control deflections have been made. **(B)** Full-left rudder and full-up stabilator have been applied but at this instant the stall break has not occurred. **(C)** The stall break has occurred, and the airplane is "free falling" as in a spin (except that in this case the path is horizontal). (From *The Flight Instructor's Manual*)

dinator) and immediately relax the wheel or briskly move it forward, *as recommended by the manufacturer.* Neutralize the rudder and start bringing in back pressure *as soon as the airspeed starts increasing* (this is important since the airplane will be pointed nearly straight down as the stall is broken), and as the pull-up is proceeding, check the airspeed for a hesitation (level flight attitude) and pick an altitude to concentrate on for leveling. (More about this in Chap. 7.)

MECHANICS OF THE SPIN

This section takes a general look at spins for many airplanes. Specifics for the Aerobat are covered as they apply.

In analyzing what to do about the spin, it would be a good idea to take a closer look at some background of the upright spin. The spin is the result of one or both wings being stalled, that is, one or both wings being past the critical angle of attack with one being deeper into the stall and having a lower coefficient of lift and higher coefficient of drag.

When you move the wheel or stick rearward and produce a stall, some interesting things may happen, depending on how the airplane is rigged and what control input exists at the time of the stall break.

At the stall break the airplane *departs*—it leaves the realm of normal, nonstalled flight. The nose may drop, and at this point the recovery may be effected by a relaxation of back pressure or a forward wheel movement, with normal flight resulting almost immediately. Or the airplane could enter a *poststall gyration,* in which nonperiodic rotation and re-pitch-up occur, again depending on control input.

The *spin* is a continued condition of stall, a step beyond the poststall gyration, with autorotation occurring.

Spin Entry. The entry (the preparation for the spin) includes clearing the area, the use of carburetor heat, the attitudes at entry, and the initial application of prospin controls. Various entries you may encounter will be discussed later in the chapter.

Incipient Spin. This is the part of the spin in which the airplane is accelerating in pitch, roll, and yaw into the developed spin. The path is changing from horizontal to vertical. The aerodynamic forces (induced by the controls and asymmetric forces on the wings and other components) are overcoming the inertia of the airplane and building up the rotation rate. For most lighter airplanes, the first *two turns* are considered the incipient phase.

Steeper modes (the nose is pointed farther down) require fewer turns to stabilize because the angle of attack doesn't have to climb so high. A modified general aviation airplane at NASA Langley took about four turns from the entry to get into the flat mode. For instance, if you decide to spin a *normal* category airplane illegally and don't get a developed spin at two or three turns, you might think there is no problem—until you keep on with your "experiments" and find an unrecoverable flat mode at four turns or so.

One demonstration your instructor may have you do later is to set up a normal power-off spin and at two turns take your hands and feet off the controls. Up to two turns, most airplanes normally recover and go into a dive. (Whoever is in charge should ease it out before the airspeed gets too high.) Trimming the airplane nose-up before starting the hands-off demonstration makes an even better point, as the airplane will recover and then ease out of its dive. You have to know the airplane before doing this.

Developed Spin. In a developed spin, the airplane has reached a constant rotation rate and pitch attitude, or a *repeatable* pattern of rotation and pitch attitudes. Some airplanes, once the spin has developed, have a steep nose-down spin with a constant rotation rate; others may be cyclic or oscillatory, with a part of each turn being steep and the rest of it in a flatter attitude. The nose bobs up and down as it rotates, and the rate of rotation changes, repeating itself within each turn or so, the rotation being faster when the nose is farthest down and slowing up when the nose rises.

Other airplanes may, in the developed spin, change attitudes and rotation rates (or have cyclic modes). A C-150 Aerobat this writer taught aerobatics in for about 800 hours had the usual incipient spin at zero to two turns and then had a steep mode with the nose well down and a fast rotation rate at three to five turns, followed by a flatter mode with the nose not so far down and a slower rotation rate in the seven- to eight-

turn area (with pro spin controls held). It then repeated these modes every few turns, each readily recoverable, but the steeper mode had an almost instantaneous recovery while the less steep took one and one-half to two turns to recover after aerodynamic recovery controls were applied. (Figs. 3-4, 3-5, and 3-6 show spin graphs of that airplane.)

For some types of airplanes there are *three indications* of the spin, going from the steep to a flatter mode: (1) the nose can be seen slowly rising as the spin progresses, (2) the sound decreases as the airplane slows in airspeed at the flatter pitch (the airspeed indicator may go from a stalling speed value of, as an example, 45 K down to 0), and (3) the pilot can feel more of a sideslip effect as the airplane does less rolling and more yawing.

In some cases the propeller may stop during this mode, but it has no effect on recovery; after the pullout, the starter is used (don't forget to shout "Clear!") to resume normal flight. What would you do if the starter was inoperative at this point? For instance, you turn the key to the starting position (the mags are still hot) and something breaks in there. As a rough figure, based on 100-HP and 150-HP trainers with midtime engines, it takes something in the vicinity of 1200 ft of altitude and 120–130 K of airspeed (IAS) to get the prop windmilling for start. Your airplane may vary either way from these numbers (Think of these as *minimums,* to be on the safe side.)

While on the subject of altitude loss, the question often comes up as to how much the average trainer loses per turn in the spin. *It depends.* For instance, for a one-turn spin, including entry, incipient spin, and recovery, you'd better plan on 1000 ft from start to finish. That may sound like a lot of altitude for a one-turn spin, but the point is that the entry and pullout take a goodly amount of altitude, which must be included in the average altitude loss of that one turn. On the other hand, a 21-turn spin in the C-150 Aerobat took 4100 ft of altitude from start to level flight again. The altitude required for one entry and pullout has much less effect in boosting total altitude as the number of turns increases (dividing 4100 by 21 gives an average of about 195 ft of altitude loss per turn).

Getting back to potential problems: If you are spinning and unexpectedly start getting one or more of the three indications mentioned, start the recovery procedure *immediately.* It's possible that a flatter mode (particularly if you had not previously encountered it or didn't know it existed for *your* airplane) could delay or even preclude recovery. *It's strongly suggested that you limit any spins to six turns or less;* that's enough to see the basics of spins and recoveries.

AUTOROTATION. To get a look at what's happening in autorotation as applied to the developed spin, let's backtrack and assume that you are going to do a deliberate, straight-ahead entry with no crossed controls and with the power at idle, so as not to complicate matters.

You have plenty of altitude, the airplane is certifi-

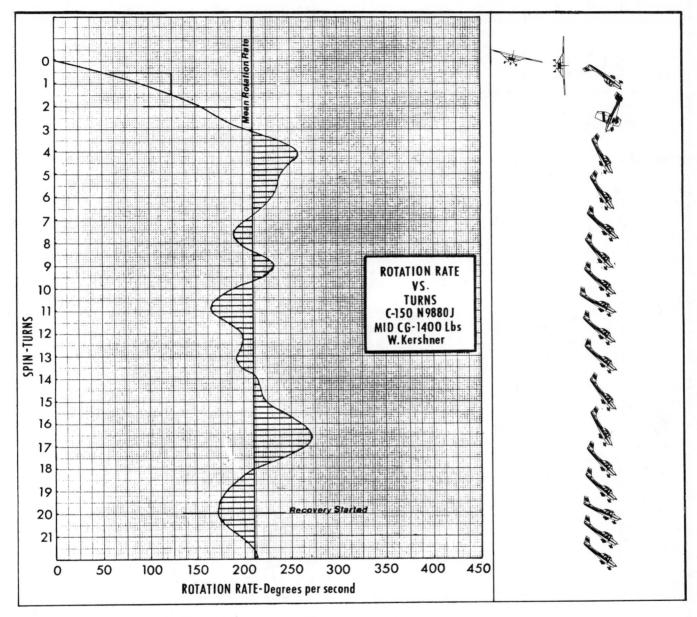

Fig. 3-4. Rotation rate versus turns for a spin in a Cessna 150 Aerobat. The airplanes on the right side of the illustration show the approximate pitch attitudes at the various turns and rotation rates. Note that for this airplane the higher the pitch attitude, the slower the rate of rotation. Figures 3-4, 3-5, and 3-6 were done as research for this book and show the reactions of a *particular* airplane. Again, it's suggested that you limit your spins to six turns or less— *your* airplane may have different spin and recovery reactions.

cated for spins, and you are over wide-open country, out of controlled airspace. You clear the area before using carburetor heat as recommended and then smoothly close the throttle, easing the nose up to a power-off, wings-level stall attitude. Assume no flaps and no ailerons are to be used.

As the stall warner goes off (and the wings are at the peak of the coefficient of lift versus angle of attack curve), lead with left rudder and move the wheel full aft

at a slightly faster rate to get a definite break. (This procedure is needed for some airplanes to ensure a good spin entry.)

The airplane yaws left; that left wing has less lift because of the relative decrease in velocity, and a roll is induced, further increasing the angle of attack. The left wing goes over the coefficient of lift peak and is stalled. Meanwhile the right wing has moved upward, *decreasing* its angle of attack, and it has more lift than the left

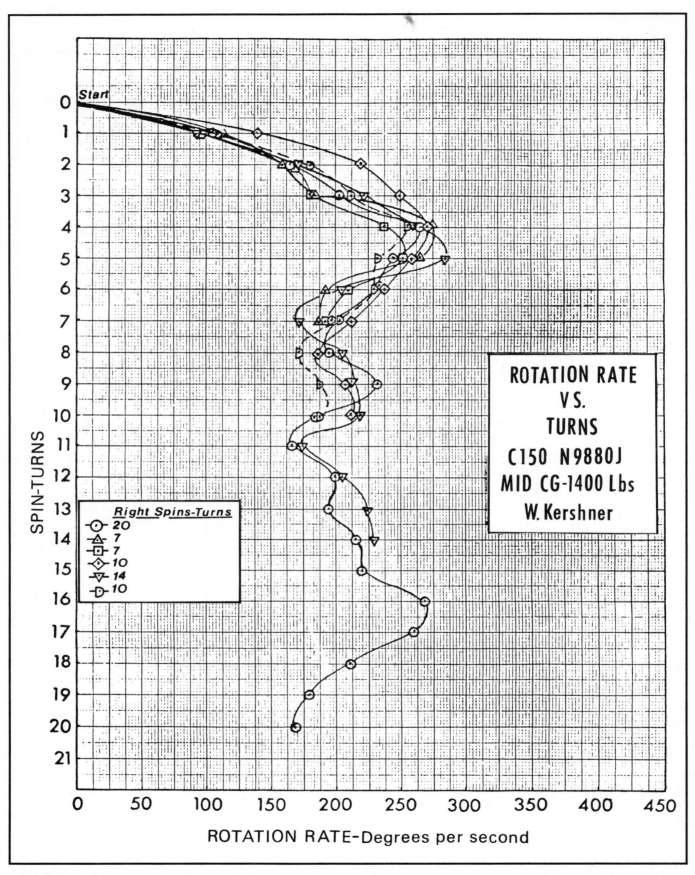

Fig. 3-5. Rotation rate versus turns (right spins) for one Cessna 150 Aerobat. The numbers by the symbols indicate the number of turns for that spin.

28

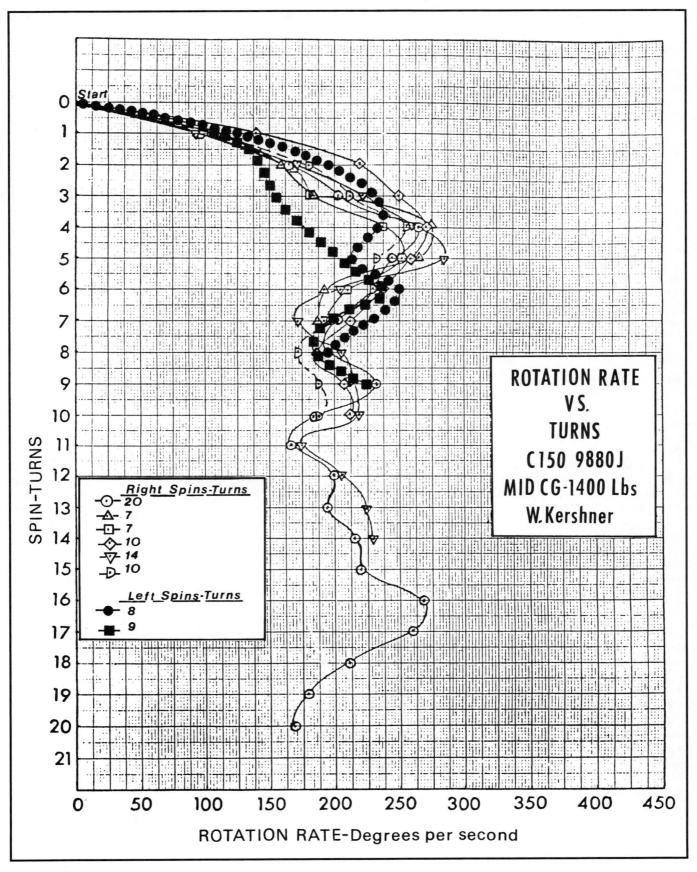

Fig. 3-6. Six right spins of Fig. 3-5 plus two left spins. Notice that for this particular airplane the rotation rates for the left spins do not increase so rapidly or attain as high a value as for the right spins. You may find that other airplanes of the same model may have different left and right spin characteristics from those shown here.

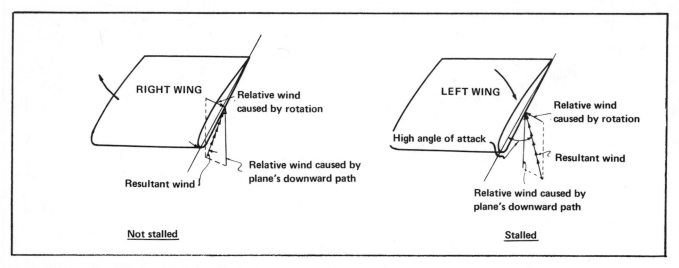

Fig. 3-7. Relative angles of attack for the wings in a left spin. The left wing has a higher angle of attack (past the stall) resulting in less lift and more drag. Autorotation is occurring. (From *The Student Pilot's Flight Manual*)

one. Fig. 3-7 gives a schematic picture of what is happening as the airplane rolls to the left and the spin develops; in a steeper spin, as illustrated, one wing is stalled and the other is basically still "flying." In flatter spin modes, both wings are well past the stall angle of attack.

In a left spin, the left wing has a *higher* coefficient of *drag* and *lower coefficient of lift* than the right, so the forces are producing autorotation, tending to keep the airplane in the spin.

Spin Recovery. Recovery is the portion of the spin process from the first input of aerodynamic controls for recovery until the autorotation and stall are broken. One pilot experienced in spins was asked if he liked an airplane that spun well, and he replied that he preferred one that *recovered* well.

The recovery on the older trainers (for example, Champion and Cub) is a three-step process: (1) Stop the autorotation by using opposite rudder so that both wings are equally stalled (at that instant the airplane isn't tending to rotate but is moving vertically downward in a straight stall, buffeting; in other words, it is still in the stalled condition even though the nose appears to be pointed straight down). (2) Relax the back pressure (or exert a brisk forward motion) on the wheel or stick so that the airplane is pointed the way it's going. (3) Then pull out of the dive. Using a model, you may see that this is also the situation in the straight-ahead stall (Fig. 3-8).

The *Pilot's Operating Handbook* for a particular airplane will *always* be the final criterion for spin recovery procedures. Here's the recommended procedure for the Aerobat (Fig. 3-9).

1. *Power off.* For many airplanes, power hurts the recovery process; the nose tends to pitch up when power is applied and stay up higher while it is on. (The new T-

tail airplanes have less reaction to power change, but this is a general approach.) A feeling is that some of the standard tail configurations with power on resist the pilot's pushing of the nose down during the recovery. (This will be looked at again.)

2. *Neutralize the ailerons.* If you are like most pilots, you're trying to stop the spin with the ailerons, as mentioned earlier in the scenario, which makes matters worse for *some* airplanes. Since you may not have thought of what ailerons do to this airplane in a spin (whether they help or hinder recovery), it's better not to take any chances—they should be neutralized.

3. *Get the flaps up.* In an inadvertent spin situation, flaps may cause poor recovery characteristics and the maximum flap-down speed may be exceeded. (More about this in Chap. 7.)

4. *Apply full rudder opposite to the rotation and hold it.* Simple enough, except there's an outside possibility that you could get confused in an accidental spin and forget which way the airplane is rotating. Sure, if you do a deliberate spin and are holding, say, full left rudder throughout the process, you should know enough to push the opposite or right rudder, but people are funny. The developed spin in that airplane may have a very fast rotation rate, and the ground may look like a blur. The direction may not be so readily discernible as

Fig. 3-8. Comparison of older- and later-model trainer spin recoveries. **(A)** The J-3 Cubs and Aeronca Champions, which were lighter per cubic foot of airplane volume (lower relative density) and had much of the mass centered near the fuselage. **(B)** Later trainers such as the C-150 and C-152, which have higher relative densities and different mass distributions (fuel tanks in the wings, extended propeller shafts, etc.).

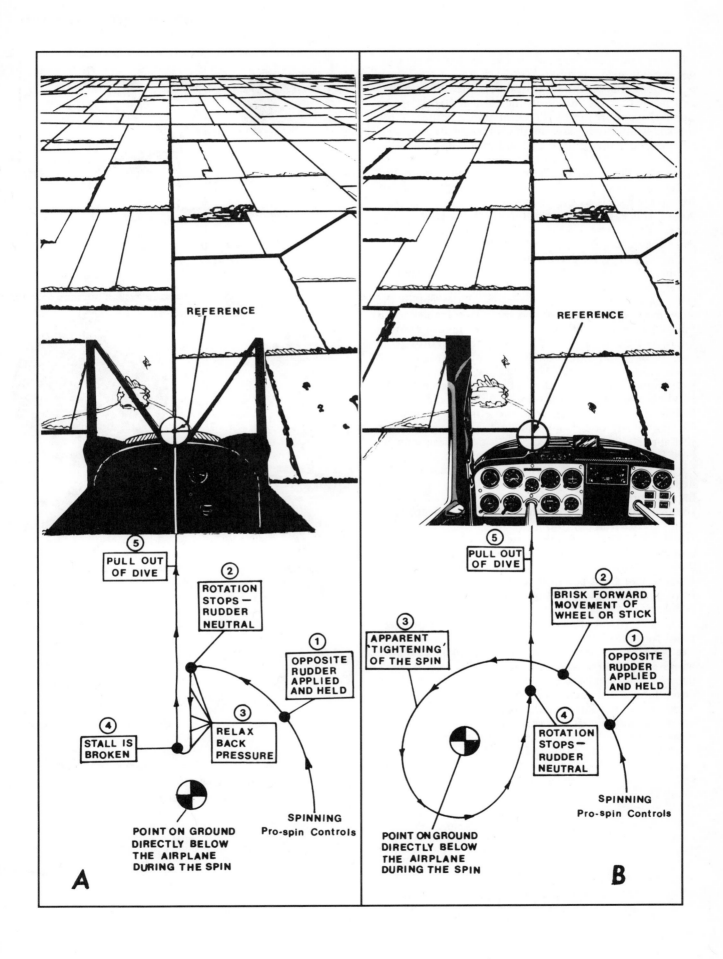

you may think, and you may not remember which rudder is being held—if any.

Again, the reference to use for turn direction, if you need it, is the needle in the turn and slip, or the small airplane in the turn coordinator. The needle (or the small airplane) leans in the direction of the spin. Apply rudder opposite to that indication and hold it.

5. *Apply brisk forward motion on the wheel or stick immediately after the application of rudder.* For some newer airplanes, the rate of application of forward wheel is as important as how far it's moved. Again, this is different from the older, lighter trainers. Some pilots are so glad to be out of the spin that they leave the nose down too long and the airspeed goes too high, with an excessive altitude loss. (Diving into the ground while congratulating yourself on a fine spin recovery is as fatal as spinning all the way in.) Incidentally, as a ballpark figure for rates of descent in the steep mode of the Aerobat and other light trainers, you might expect 7000–8000 fpm; in flatter modes the rate might fall off to a mere 5000 fpm or so. Hitting the ground at either rate would dent your airplane. The steep mode is primarily roll, the flat mode primarily yaw. Some pilots hold the opposite rudder after the rotation stops and start a spin in the other direction (a progressive spin), which requires a new recovery, including using rudder opposite to the opposite rudder just applied, which can be as confusing as this sentence.

The back pressure is sometimes relaxed too much (or the wheel is moved forward too abruptly past the neutral position), and you get light in your seat. If it happens unexpectedly you could think that the airplane suddenly has undesirable characteristics. You probably won't realize that *you* did it.

6. *When the rotation stops, neutralize the rudder and pull out of the dive.* Ease the airplane out of the dive. Don't get a secondary stall but don't dally either, since airspeed will be building up at a fast rate. Expect to pull between 2½ and 3 g's during the pullout.

Fig. 3-10A–I shows a spin from entry to recovery in an Aerobat (N9880J).

As a *general* rule, the steeper the spin attitude, the more easily the recovery is effected. Some pilots don't like the steeper modes because they are looking at the ground in a (to them) vertical, nose-down attitude. They prefer the flatter modes because yawing motions are apparently not as balance-disturbing as rolling motions.

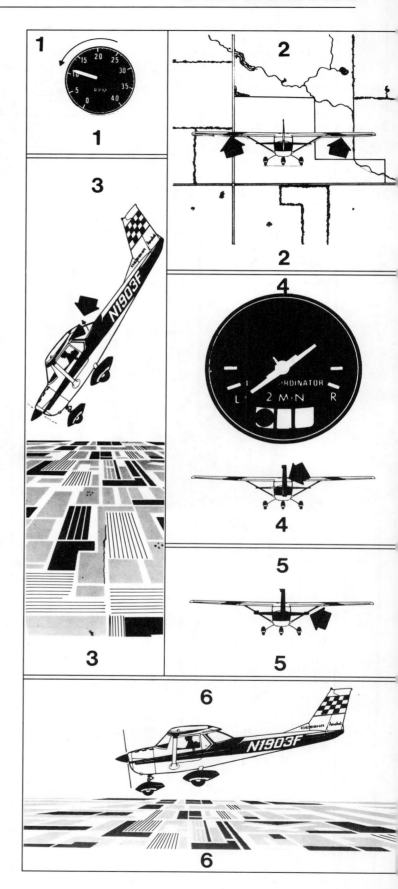

Fig. 3-9. Steps recommended for spin recovery in the Aerobat. **(1)** Close the throttle. **(2)** Neutralize the ailerons. **(3)** Get the flaps up (if they are down in an inadvertent spin). **(4)** Apply full rudder opposite to the rotation. **(5)** Apply brisk forward motion on the wheel. **(6)** Neutralize the rudder and pull out of the dive. (More details about various models later in the chapter.)

Fig. 3-10A-I. Spin from entry to recovery in an Aerobat (N9880J).

(A) The wheel was moved full aft and right rudder applied as the stall warner sounded. The airplane is rolling and yawing to the right. A blast of power is used to help get the spin started, then the throttle is closed.

(B) The airplane has rolled to the vertical as the nose has moved approximately 45° from the original heading.

(C) After about 90° of heading change the airplane is in an inverted position.

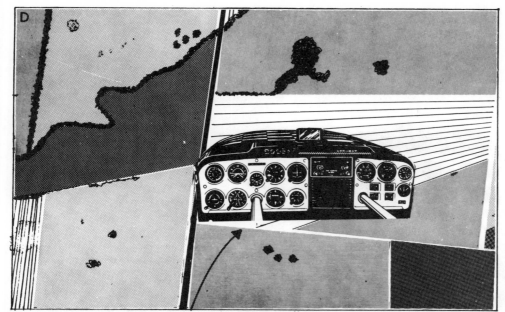

(D) The airplane is approaching a near-vertical, nose-down attitude.

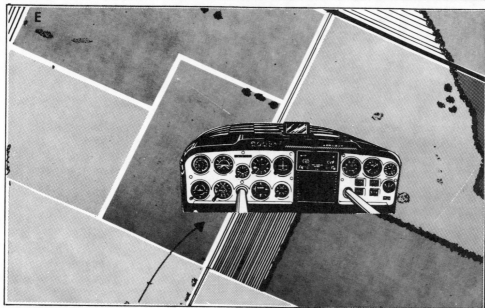

(E) The airplane is moving into the steeper mode of the developed spin, the rate of rotation increasing rapidly.

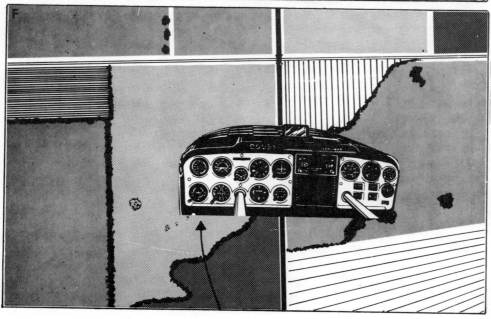

(F) The developed right spin at about the five-turn point in Figs. 3-4, 3-5, and 3-6.

(G) The nose has moved up to a flatter attitude, and the prop is stopping. This would be at about the seven- to eight-turn point in Figs. 3-4, 3-5, and 3-6.

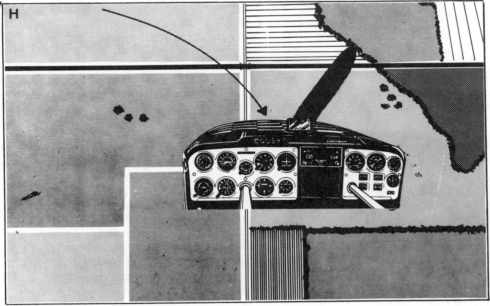

(H) No power is being developed (obviously). Check that the ailerons are neutral. Use full opposite (left) rudder, followed by brisk forward movement of the wheel. When the rotation stops (it may take a turn or two in the less-steep attitudes), neutralize the rudder and pull out of the dive.

(I) After level flight attitude is reached, start the engine. (Clear!)

During the recovery from a flatter mode, pilots may be disturbed by the nose dropping and the rotation rate apparently increasing. Actually, it is normally a good sign; the airplane is going back through the steep mode as it moves toward recovery. Not realizing this, they could release the control application, thinking the spin is getting worse, and thereby delay the actual recovery (look at Fig. 3-8B again).

However, an airplane certificated for spins usually moves through this stage in the recovery so rapidly that the pilot doesn't have time to react anyway.

One problem with pilots inexperienced in spins is that they may apply the proper control, but after a half turn (or one turn) with no apparent recovery, they become anxious and may ease off the deflection to try something else since the recommended recovery "didn't work." They try different combinations, hoping for the best, which naturally delays any recovery. Even a pilot with much experience who is used to the near-instant recoveries from the incipient phase (zero to two turns) of the current trainers may be taken aback in a developed spin by the fact that instead of an eighth turn, quarter turn, or half turn, it may take one or two turns before good things start happening. The first time this occurs, the surprise may cause the pilot to back off and try something—anything—else, with a cost of time and altitude, particularly altitude.

An improper recovery procedure could mean a delay in stopping the spin. Maybe the opposite rudder was not put to the stop and/or the wheel or stick was moved ahead slowly or halfheartedly. A good move in this case is to go prospin controls again (rudder with the spin) wheel full back) to get a running start in using the controls for recovery. Rapid and full opposite rudder followed quickly by a brisk forward movement of the wheel, *and held,* is an effective recovery move.

RECOVERY SUMMARY. To review, the best *all-around* recovery procedure is to apply full opposite rudder followed immediately (or one-fourth to one turn later, depending on the manufacturer's recommendations) by brisk forward movement—maybe to full forward (as required with aft centers of gravity)—of the stick or control wheel. Again, this does not replace the specific techniques outlined by the manufacturer of a particular airplane.

Other Spin Factors. Remember, *if an airplane is hard to get into a spin, it could be even more difficult to get out.* For example, assume that the angle of attack of a particular airplane (clean) is 16° when the stall occurs. This is not such a large angle, and only a small area of the fin and rudder may be blanketed by the horizontal tail as the spin is entered. Also assume that the rudder power is weak even at this low angle and the pilot barely has enough yaw force available to get the spin started.

As the spin develops it gets into a flatter mode where the angle of attack is 45° or more. (Look at some of the airplane attitudes—and angles of attack—in Fig. 3-4.) Even more of the rudder, which is a vital recovery control for the majority of general aviation airplanes, is blanketed by the horizontal tail wake, and it may not be effective for breaking the built-up forces of inertia.

Don't spin an airplane that you know is in the normal category, even if a placard against spins isn't visible. (The placard could have fallen off the panel and disappeared, and in any case the manufacturer of a normal-category airplane is only required to demonstrate a one-turn spin or a three-second spin, whichever is longer, with a recovery being effected within one turn after normal antispin controls are applied.) To repeat, the *incipient spin normally* consists of the first two turns after prospin controls are used. Considering that criterion, you can see that the FAA doesn't require the manufacturer to demonstrate a *developed* spin for certification in the normal category. And manufacturers of multiengine airplanes aren't required to do anything concerning spins!

Don't deliberately spin an airplane that has a big fat placard against spins. If you do it and get out of a well-developed spin, write or call the manufacturer and tell how you did it.

Another point: *Check all cable tensions to ensure full recovery control.* The fact that control cables may have slackened since the airplane came from the factory is often overlooked.

One problem with spins is that the airplane is operating in an area of aerodynamics—past the stall—where predictions of performance are extremely difficult. At higher angles of attack airflow separation on the wings and tail and at junctions of these components with the fuselage cause headaches for manufacturers.

The sooner you move to recover, the better off you will be. During the general aviation airplane spin program at NASA-Langley it was indicated that all configurations tested, even those that *had unrecoverable flat spins when fully developed,* recovered from a one-turn spin within one additional turn (emphasis added). The unrecoverable spins referred to were those that required the deployment of the antispin parachute for recovery. The normal aerodynamic controls were not sufficient for spin recovery under certain loadings and configurations of the test airplane.

Don't ever spin any airplane with people or baggage in the back. A rearward center of gravity could mean that the spin could be unrecoverable. The developed spin with a rearward center of gravity is normally flatter, and the controls may be ineffective for recovery.

You may have questions concerning inverted spins, and your instructor should make it clear that the airplane's attitude at entry has nothing to do with whether the spin will settle down to be normal or inverted. The usual fear is that if the airplane is stalled in the inverted position, a resulting spin will always be inverted. If the stall is the result of moving the wheel back toward the pilot and holding it there, however, the spin will settle down to be a normal one even if the whole process was started while inverted at the top of a loop. (This requires that you continue to hold rudder and up-elevator—otherwise the spin could turn into a spiral.) If the prespin stall is a result of the control wheel or stick being moved *forward,* the spin will be inverted even though the airplane was in an upright flight attitude at the time (getting into an inverted spin from an upright attitude is unlikely, even though it could happen). An inverted spin is more likely to begin with the airplane in a nose-high, inverted attitude, as at the top of a sloppy Immelmann with excessive abuse of forward elevator and rudder input.

Various Spin Entries. The straight-ahead, power-off entry is not the usual way an accidental spin happens. Your instructor may demonstrate over-the-top and under-the-bottom entries (explaining under what circumstances each could occur and also demonstrate and let you practice upright (positive-g) spins from the top of loops or spins resulting from "extended" snap rolls. Another good demonstration in some airplanes is a "feet-on-the-floor" spin entry.

The point of these various types of entries is to show that the *recovery* is basically the same for the developed upright spin. Pilots don't realize that after a certain number of turns most airplanes have forgotten just how they got into a spin. Even with an entry from a snap roll, after two or three turns the airplane settles down to a normal spin (assuming that the throttle was closed after the snap started).

It's assumed in every case that the airplane is properly certificated and loaded, a pilot qualified in spinning this *airplane is aboard, you have plenty of altitude, and you clear the area before each spin entry.*

OVER-THE-TOP ENTRY. This is the stall in which the higher wing in a bank stalls first. In this case you get into the spin by injudiciously holding top rudder (and maybe a little aileron into the bank, to help the slip) as back pressure is used. You'll normally get a better demonstration by turning to the right with power on.

Hold the wheel or stick back as the airplane rolls and the high wing drops. Apply *full* rudder into the spin if it wasn't in all the way, neutralize the ailerons, and close the throttle smoothly. Hold it in the spin for about a turn and a half and then use normal recovery procedures.

One problem with this entry is that you are carrying a high power setting (because it's often difficult to get a good spin entry over the top from idle), and when you close the throttle you may get rapid engine cooling. You don't want to be carrying carburetor heat at climb power at the beginning—this is bad also for an engine. Work out a system for your airplane that helps take care of the engine and still gives a good spin entry.

UNDER-THE-BOTTOM ENTRY. This is basically a continuation of the cross-controlled stall (rudder into the turn, aileron against). After the stall break and roll,

neutralize the ailerons, close the throttle, and allow about a one-and-one-half-turn spin. Use the standard recovery. Doing the spin to the left and carrying some power usually helps the entry. Although flaps would be used on an actual approach, *deliberate* spins with flaps extended are usually prohibited by the manufacturer because of adverse recovery characteristics; also, the flap-extended speed could be exceeded with the flaps down, if somebody isn't quick to get them up.

NO-RUDDER ENTRY. The common belief is that the rudder is the only control that can develop the spin, Pilots may get complacent about its use, figuring that as long as they don't use the rudder too much in the stall regime, they're okay. In a takeoff and departure stall the pilot may try to raise a wing with aileron alone and get this problem.

ENTRY FROM A LOOP. The instructor may demonstrate spinning (or have you spin) the airplane from the top of a loop at some time during the training so you'll know what will happen if you pull back too hard to "tighten it up." The spin will be an upright one even if the airplane goes through some wild gyrations before settling down.

Fly a normal loop and as the airplane becomes inverted pull the stick or wheel all the way back while moving in with full (left or right) rudder. Agree beforehand that the instructor will say "NOW" or something like that when you are to start to spin. Things happen so fast in the loop that you'll have to apply prospin controls without delay. Hold this control input so that a spin occurs. For recovery, close the throttle, neutralize the ailerons, and use normal procedures.

SNAP-TYPE ENTRY. This one usually occurs when you are late in applying recovery controls in a snap roll (with cruise or climb power). The airplane continues the roll with the nose gradually dropping as the spin progresses.

You'll note in most cases that the power is tending to keep the nose up, and the first turn or so can make you think that the airplane is going to stay flat.

Close the throttle, make sure the ailerons are neutral, and make a normal recovery.

Hands-off recovery. As indicated earlier, a good demonstration of *recovery* would be to set up a power-off, wings-level spin entry and at one to two turns quickly remove hands and feet from the controls. (Count the turns and let go at "TWO" or "NOW.") The response of one airplane, hands off, at two turns in a left spin is a movement of the control wheel to the left (the airplane gives itself left aileron) and then a recentering of the wheel as it moves forward and the spin recovery is completed. As noted, if the airplane is trimmed slightly nose-up before the spin, it will pull out of the following dive by itself after the recovery. You'll then adjust power and trim for cruise, climb, etc. It's a good confidence builder if done properly and shows that in the incipient spin you are better off letting go rather than holding the wheel full back.

Spin Summary in General. An airplane's spin characteristics still cannot be predicted as well as other areas of performance, or stability and control. If you do spins you should adhere strictly to the manufacturers' recommendations. There is nothing worse than deciding on the spur of the moment to get into a spin situation where you haven't been and to discover that the airplane isn't responding to the recovery controls as it did before. That extra turn or two (or more) for recovery can take a very long time. Again, do spins with an instructor who has experience in the airplane you are using before trying solo spins in it.

MORE ABOUT SPINNING THE AEROBAT

Cessna Aircraft Company has published a booklet, *Spin Characteristics of Cessna Models 150, A150, 152, A152, 172, R172, and 177.* The 150 and 152 models are the ones discussed here. The following information and good advice are from that booklet.

The subject of airplane spinning is a complex one, which is often over-simplified during hangar-flying sessions. There are increasing numbers of pilots, including flight instructors, who, because of the structure of present pilot certification requirements, have had little or no training in spins and spin recovery. This has resulted in some confusion and misunderstanding over the behavior of airplanes in spinning flight, and it appears that this lack of understanding may have contributed to some serious accidents. In the interest of expanding each pilot's knowledge and increasing the safety of his operations, we will discuss some factors influencing spin behavior as it pertains to the Cessna Models 150, A150, 152, and A152 which are approved for intentional spins.

The following list summarizes important safety points relative to the performance of intentional spins.

BASIC GUIDELINES FOR INTENTIONAL SPINS
(1) KNOW YOUR AIRCRAFT THOROUGHLY.
(2) PRIOR TO DOING SPINS IN ANY MODEL AIRCRAFT, OBTAIN THOROUGH INSTRUCTION IN SPINS FROM AN INSTRUCTOR FULLY QUALIFIED AND CURRENT IN SPINNING *THAT MODEL.*
(3) BE FAMILIAR WITH THE PARACHUTE, AIRSPACE AND WEATHER REQUIREMENTS OF FAR 91 AS AFFECT YOUR FLIGHT.
(4) CHECK THE AIRCRAFT WEIGHT AND BALANCE TO BE SURE YOU ARE WITHIN THE APPROVED ENVELOPE FOR SPINS.
(5) SECURE OR REMOVE ALL LOOSE COCKPIT EQUIPMENT PRIOR TO TAKEOFF.
(6) BE SURE THE AREA TO BE USED IS SUITABLE FOR SPINS AND IS CLEAR OF OTHER TRAFFIC.
(7) ENTER EACH SPIN AT A HIGH ALTITUDE. PLAN RECOVERIES TO BE COMPLETED *WELL ABOVE* THE MINIMUM LEGAL ALTITUDE OF 1500 FEET ABOVE THE SURFACE.
(8) CONDUCT ALL ENTRIES IN ACCORDANCE WITH THE PROCEDURES RECOMMENDED BY THE MANUFACTURER.
(9) LIMIT YOURSELF TO 2-TURN SPINS UNTIL COMPLETELY FAMILIAR WITH THE CHARACTERISTICS OF YOUR AIRPLANE.
(10) USE THE FOLLOWING RECOVERY PROCEDURES FOR THE CESSNA MODELS 150, A150, 152 AND A152.
  (a) VERIFY THAT AILERONS ARE NEUTRAL AND THROTTLE IS IN IDLE POSITION.
  (b) APPLY AND *HOLD* RUDDER OPPOSITE TO THE DIRECTION OF ROTATION.
  (c) JUST *AFTER* THE RUDDER REACHES THE STOP, MOVE THE CONTROL WHEEL *BRISKLY* FORWARD FAR ENOUGH TO BREAK THE STALL. Full down elevator may be required at aft center of gravity loadings in some airplane models to assure optimum recoveries.
  (d) *HOLD* THESE CONTROL INPUTS UNTIL ROTATION STOPS. Premature relaxation of the control inputs may extend the recovery.
  (e) AS THE ROTATION STOPS NEUTRALIZE RUDDER AND MAKE A SMOOTH RECOVERY FROM THE RESULTING DIVE.

For the purpose of this discussion, we will divide the spin into three distinct phases. These are the entry, incipient, and steady, or developed, phases. [These are illustrated in Fig. 3-11.] The basic cause of a spin is a difference in lift and drag between the two wings with the airplane operating in essentially stalled flight. Entry to this condition is initiated, intentionally or otherwise, when the airplane is stalled in uncoordinated flight. This causes one wing to reach a higher angle of attack than the other. Beyond stall angles of attack, lift begins decreasing while drag rises rapidly. This causes a sustained autorotation to begin because of the decreased lift and increased drag of one wing half as compared to the other.

Here, in the entry phase, recovery from or prevention of the spin is as simple as normal stall recovery since, in fact, at this point that's all we are really faced with. Coordinated use of rudder and aileron to oppose any tendency to roll should be applied with emphasis on the rudder due to its generally more powerful influence at this point. This should be accompanied by relaxation of elevator back pressure to reduce the angle of attack below that of the stall. Coordinated use of all controls should then be applied to return to normal level flight. During this entry phase, recovery of control (or prevention of loss of control) will normally be instantaneous for all practical purposes as soon as the stall is broken.

The incipient phase covers that period of time from the spin entry to the fully stabilized spin. During this period the yaw being produced by a deflected rudder while the airplane is stalled is supplemented by the differences in lift and drag between the two wing panels. These parameters cause the rotating motion of the airplane to begin to increase [Fig. 3-7].

During this incipient phase, spin recoveries in those airplanes approved for intentional spins are usually rapid, and, in some airplanes, may occur merely by

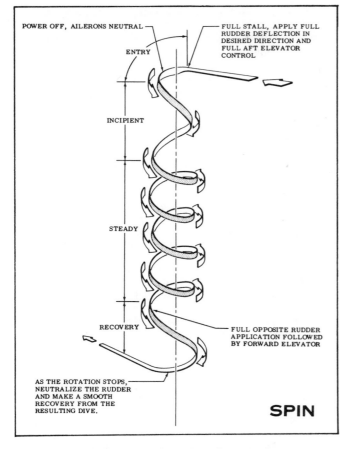

POWER OFF, AILERONS NEUTRAL

ENTRY

INCIPIENT

STEADY

RECOVERY

FULL STALL, APPLY FULL RUDDER DEFLECTION IN DESIRED DIRECTION AND FULL AFT ELEVATOR CONTROL

FULL OPPOSITE RUDDER APPLICATION FOLLOWED BY FORWARD ELEVATOR

AS THE ROTATION STOPS, NEUTRALIZE THE RUDDER AND MAKE A SMOOTH RECOVERY FROM THE RESULTING DIVE.

SPIN

Fig. 3-11. Spin phases. (From *Spin Characteristics of Cessna Models 150, A150, 152, A152, 172, R172, and 177*)

Aileron variation from neutral can cause a different balance between the aerodynamic, inertia and gyroscopic forces and cause some delay in recoveries. Typically even a slight inadvertent aileron deflection in the direction of the spin will speed up rotation and delay recoveries. Moving the elevator control forward while maintaining pro-spin rudder deflection may not provide a recovery with some airplanes. In fact, reversing the sequence of rudder-elevator inputs or even just slow, rather than brisk, inputs may lengthen recoveries. Finally, it is *important,* particularly in this steady spin phase, in addition to using the correct control applications and proper sequence of control application, to HOLD THIS APPLICATION UNTIL THE RECOVERY OCCURS. In extreme cases, this may require a full turn or more with full down elevator deflection.

The proper recovery control inputs to obtain optimum recovery characteristics in Cessna single engine airplanes approved for spins are repeated here and amplified somewhat from those listed under the incipient phase.

(1) VERIFY THAT AILERONS ARE NEUTRAL AND THROTTLE IS IN IDLE POSITION.
(2) APPLY AND *HOLD* FULL RUDDER OPPOSITE TO THE DIRECTION OF ROTATION.
(3) JUST *AFTER* THE RUDDER REACHES THE STOP, MOVE THE CONTROL WHEEL *BRISKLY* FORWARD FAR ENOUGH TO BREAK THE STALL. Full down elevator may be required at aft center of gravity loadings in some airplane models to assure optimum recoveries.
(4) *HOLD* THESE CONTROL INPUTS UNTIL ROTATION STOPS. Premature relaxation of the control inputs may extend the recovery.
(5) AS THE ROTATION STOPS NEUTRALIZE RUDDER AND MAKE A SMOOTH RECOVERY FROM THE RESULTING DIVE.

The emphasis added to these steps differentiates the steady phase from the incipient phase. The most important difference in the steady phase is an increase in the length of recoveries in this phase for some airplanes, and to a lesser extent the amount of control input needed. Up to a full turn or more to recover is not unusual in this phase. Full down elevator deflection will sometimes be needed to assure optimum recoveries at aft loadings in some airplanes. Therefore IT IS VERY IMPORTANT TO APPLY THE RECOVERY CONTROLS IN THE PROPER SEQUENCE AND THEN *HOLD* THEM UNTIL RECOVERY OCCURS.

Some of the additional factors which have (or may have) an effect on spin behavior and spin recovery characteristics are aircraft loading (distribution, center of gravity and weight), altitude, power and rigging.

Distribution of the weight of the airplane can have a significant effect on spin behavior. The addition of weight at any distance from the center of gravity of the airplane will increase its moment of inertia about two axes. This increased inertia independent of the center of gravity location or weight will tend to promote a less steep spin attitude and more sluggish recoveries. Forward location of the CG will usually make it more difficult to obtain a pure spin due to the reduced elevator effectiveness. If a spiral is encountered as evidenced

relaxing the pro-spin rudder and elevator deflections. However, positive spin recovery control inputs should be used regardless of the phase of the spin during which recovery is initiated. Briefly, these control inputs should be 1) neutral ailerons and power off, 2) full rudder opposite to the direction of rotation, 3) just after the rudder reaches the stop, elevator briskly forward to break the stall, and 4) as rotation stops, neutralize the controls and recover from the resulting dive. Using these procedures, recoveries are typically accomplished in from ⅛ to ½ turn during the incipient phase.

The final phase is the fully developed "steady" phase. Here, a more-or-less steady state spin results where the autorotational aerodynamic forces (yaw due to rudder deflection, lift and drag differences across the stalled wing) are balanced by the centrifugal and gyroscopic forces on the airframe produced by rotating motion. Due to the attitude of the airplane in a spin the total motion is made up of rolling and usually pitching motions as well as the predominate yawing motions. Movement of the airplane flight controls affects the rate of motion about one of the axes. Because of the strong gyroscopic influences in the spin, improper aerodynamic control inputs can have an adverse effect on the spin motion.

by a steady increase in airspeed and "g" loads on the airplane, recovery should be accomplished quickly by leveling the wings and recovering from the resulting dive. Conversely, extremely aft CG locations will tend to promote lengthened recoveries since a more complete stall can be achieved. Changes in airplane gross weight as well as its distribution can have an effect on spin behavior since increases in gross weight will increase inertia. Higher weights may extend recoveries slightly.

High altitudes will tend to lengthen recoveries since the less dense air provides less "bite" for the controls to oppose the spin. However, this does *not* suggest the use of low altitudes for spin practice.

Airplane rigging can have a strong influence on spin characteristics. Improper elevator and rudder deflection stops can alter the depth of entry into a spin and also can alter the amount of travel available at the control surface and may thus reduce the control power available for either entry to an intentional spin or recovery.

Power can affect the spinning attitude. If power is carried in the spin the airplane attitude may be less nose down. In addition the propeller will tend to add some gyroscopic inputs which will be reversed between left and right spins. The effect of leaving power on during a spin may lengthen recoveries on some airplanes.

The foregoing areas have been considered in the design and certification of an airplane. If the airplane is maintained and operated within manufacturers' approved limitations, the spin characteristics and recoveries will be acceptable although the trends mentioned above may be evident.

The next several paragraphs will briefly describe the typical spin characteristics of recent Cessna models approved for spins.

150F THROUGH 150L AND A150K THROUGH A150L

Entries at an aft CG will be positive from a power of unaccelerated stall. At more forward CG locations, a slightly higher deceleration rate may be necessary.

The incipient phase rotation will be rapid and the nose will progress to an average 60° to 70° nose down attitude in the vicinity of two turns.

At aft CG loadings at 2½ to 3 turns as the airplane enters the steady phase, there may be evident some change in character of the spin. The nose attitude may become less steep and rise to approximately 45° to 50° below the horizon. In addition some change in sideslip will be felt and rotation rates will change some. As the CG is moved forward this tendency to change character will disappear and spiral tendencies may appear.

Recoveries during the entry and incipient phases will vary from ¼ to ½ turn typically at aft CG loadings to practically instantaneous at forward CG loadings. Recoveries from extended spins will vary from in excess of a full turn at aft CG to ½ turn typically at forward CG locations.

CESSNA 150M AND A150M

Spin characteristics for this model are similar to those of the earlier models except as follows. Entries at forward CG loadings will be more difficult to accomplish without more rapid deceleration.

The incipient phase will be almost the same as for the older models but the character change upon entering the stable phase will be subdued but still evident at aft CG loadings. The nose attitude change may not be evident at all, although some variation in rotation rate and sideslip may be noted.

Recoveries will be similar to those of the earlier models from all phases although a slight reduction in recovery turns (⅛ to ¼) may be evident.

CESSNA 152 AND A152

Positive entries can be made from all CG locations by leading with full rudder in the desired spin direction just prior to full up elevator application.

In the incipient phase, nose attitude may cycle beyond vertical during the first turn. The rotation rate accelerates quite rapidly during the first two turns, and the nose progresses to an average 60° to 75° nose down attitude in the vicinity of two turns.

A change in turn rate may be noted in some spins beyond 2 turns with an approximate frequency of one cycle per turn (speeds up and slows down once each turn). The increase in turn rate is sometimes accompanied by aileron control forces in the direction of the spin (5 to 10 pounds). It is important that the pilot counteract these forces by holding the aileron control in the neutral position. Even small amounts of aileron deflection with the spin may increase the rotation rate and prolong the recovery.

Spiral tendencies may be evident at the forward CG loadings as noted by light elevator buffet, an increase in airspeed beyond 80 KIAS, and a steadily increasing "g" load.

Recoveries during the first two turns may take somewhat more than ½ turn typically at aft CG loadings to ¼ turn or less at forward CG loadings. Recoveries from extended spins will vary from in excess of a full turn at aft CG to 1 turn or less at forward CG locations.

For the purpose of training in spins and spin recoveries, a 1 or 2 turn spin will normally provide all that is necessary. All of the characteristic motions and control inputs required will have been experienced. Longer spins, while acceptable as a maneuver in appropriately certified airplanes, provide little additional insight to a student in the area of spin recovery since the prime reason for conducting a spin is to learn how to avoid an inadvertent entry in the first place and then how to recover if one should develop.

It is recommended that, where feasible, entries be accomplished at altitudes high enough to complete recoveries 4000 feet or more above ground level. At least 1000 feet of altitude loss should be allowed for a 1 turn spin and recovery, while a 6 turn spin and recovery may require somewhat more than twice that amount for the Cessna Models 150, A150, 152, and A152. For example, the recommended entry altitude for a 6 turn spin should be 6000 feet above ground level. In any case, entries should be planned so that recoveries are completed well above the minimum 1500 feet above ground level required by FAR 91.

Another reason for using high altitudes for practicing spins is that a greater field of view is provided which will assist in maintaining pilot orientation. However, if disorientation does occur and precludes a visual turn determination of the direction of rotation, the symbolic airplane of the turn coordinator or the needle of the turn and bank indicator (not the ball) may be referred to for this information.

Finally, a pilot planning to spin a new model for the first time or after a long absence from this type of maneuver should first fly with a qualified instructor pilot who can point out key points in the spin and recovery process for this particular type of airplane. The weight and balance should be checked carefully to assure that the spins will be conducted at an approved loading. As previously stated, plenty of altitude should be maintained at all times. *Information Manual* procedures for the spin and spin recovery should be rigorously followed for the optimum and most repeatable characteristics.

4

BASIC AEROBATIC MANEUVERS

THE THREE FUNDAMENTALS

The three basic maneuvers — the roll, loop, and snap roll—are to aerobatic flying what the Four Fundamentals (turns, climbs, glides, and straight and level) are to everyday flying. Nearly every aerobatic maneuver is a variation or combination of these. Get these Three Fundamentals well established, both in theory and technique, and there won't be problems with maneuvers such as the Cuban eight or Immelmann.

THE AILERON ROLL

The aileron roll, when done properly, is one of the most beautiful and graceful maneuvers in aerobatic flying (Fig. 4-1).

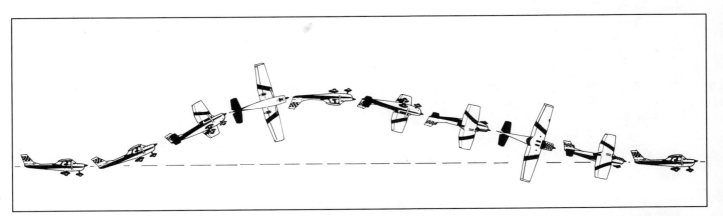

Fig. 4-1. Aileron roll.

The airplane is rolled about the longitudinal axis, using coordinated controls, and as the name implies, the ailerons are the primary control for this maneuver. (The airplane is also moving with respect to the vertical and lateral axes.) A real reference on the horizon is used to start the maneuver, and the nose appears to project a very tight orbit about an imaginary point about 10° to the left (left roll) as the roll progresses.

This is a very good maneuver for building your confidence and coordination. (Your probable reaction after the first good one you do will be one of relief and confidence that it *is* possible to roll an airplane around to a normal attitude after it has been on its back even for a short while.) You will feel better about your chances of getting out of a sticky situation of wake turbulence if the airplane gets inverted, but you should realize that the roll rate of wake turbulence may exceed the roll rate of a general aviation airplane. So, you'd still better avoid wake turbulence if possible, even if you turn out to be the hottest "aileron roller" in the business. More about this later.

The aileron roll has the advantage of being a simple, seemingly spectacular, easy-on-the-body maneuver with no negative g's or excess positive forces. You should, for instance, pull a maximum of +2 g's (in the C-150 Aerobat; 2.5 g's is suggested for the C-152) on the pull-up to entry and then maintain +1 g throughout the roll.

PROCEDURE IN THE AILERON ROLL. Fig. 4-2A–H shows the aileron roll in sequence.

In level flight, set the power at cruise airspeed (80–90 K) to 2300 rpm (2500 rpm) to help avoid overspeed at the recommended entry speed of 115 K (130 mph).

Pick a reference point on the horizon and line up the nose with it. After making sure that *the area is clear,* ease the nose over to obtain the recommended entry speed. Assume the roll will be made to the left.

Pull the nose up smoothly (wings level) to 30° above the horizon. Relax the back pressure slightly to maintain this pitch attitude as you start applying left aileron and rudder as if entering a steep turn (Fig. 4-2A). Continue to increase the aileron deflection rapidly (but smoothly) until the maximum is obtained.

When the airplane rolls past a 45° bank, use less rudder to avoid pulling the nose down below the horizon (pulling it off-heading) (Fig. 4-2B). As 90° of roll is passed, start *relaxing the back pressure* more. The ailerons are still fully deflected and the back pressure remains relaxed (Fig. 4-2C).

As the airplane reaches the *inverted position,* nearly but not all back pressure has been released in an attempt to keep the nose above the horizon (Fig. 4-2D). The nose gradually moves down as the maneuver progresses, even with no back pressure. (Had the initial back pressure needed to pull the nose *up* been continued, the nose would have been "pulled" down well below the horizon as the airplane approached the inverted position.)

Figs. 4-2E and 4-2F show the roll continuing past

Fig. 4-2A-H. Aileron roll attitudes as seen from the cockpit and from behind the airplane. (Imagine that in the illustrations on the right you are in a following airplane, matching the roll.)

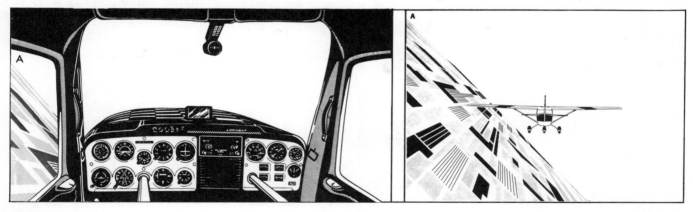

(A) 45° of roll.

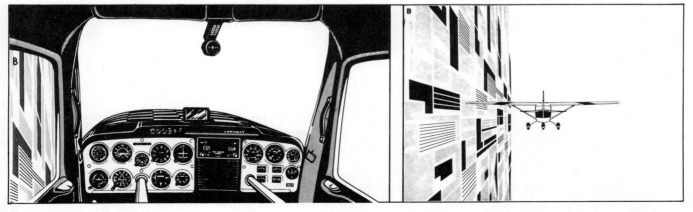

(B) 90° of roll.

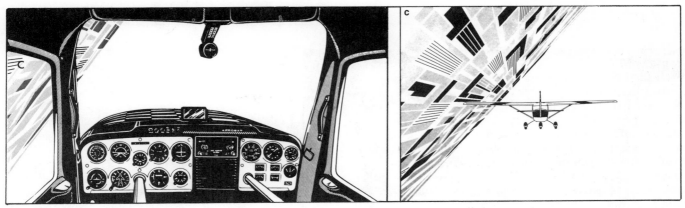

(C) 135° of roll.

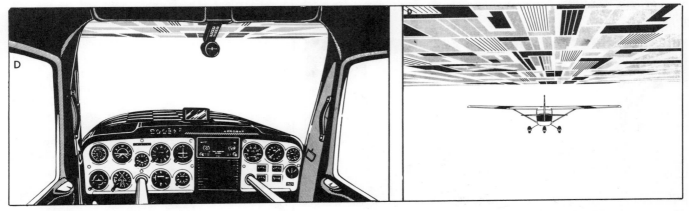

(D) 180° of roll — fully inverted.

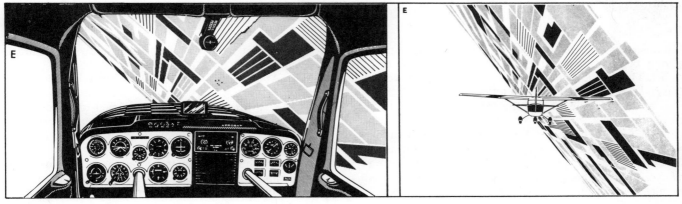

(E) 225° of roll.

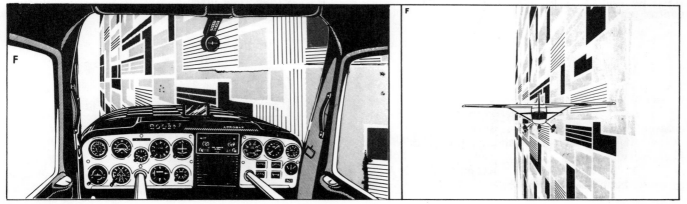

(F) 270° of roll.

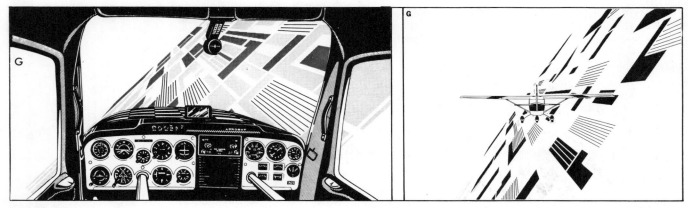

(G) 315° of roll.

(H) 360° of roll—wings-level, normal cruising flight. The roll portion should take about 6 seconds in the Aerobat.

the inverted position. A common error is to start reapplying back pressure at the 270° of roll point (Fig. 4-2F). This is one cause of ending up headed off well to the *right* of the reference in a left roll.

As the airplane reaches the 45° bank (315° of roll), now start *back pressure* slowly and smoothly again (Fig. 4-2G). At this point, reapply sufficient left rudder with that back pressure to keep the nose from dropping. The airspeed value will be lower than earlier in the maneuver, so use more rudder deflection to get the desired result. Fig. 4-4 and the accompanying text will expain the why of this.

Hold full aileron deflection from the start of the roll until time to recover. A summation of probable control usage during the aileron roll to the left follows:

1. Initial pull-up—back pressure only. (Relax as necessary to maintain the proper pitch attitude.)
2. Start of the roll—slight back pressure, left aileron, and left rudder. (Continue to increase aileron deflection.)
3. At 45° of roll—full aileron, rudder pressure decreasing slightly, slight back pressure.
4. At 90° of roll—full aileron, little rudder, less back pressure.
5. At 180° of roll—full aileron, very little back pressure, light rudder pressure.

6. At 270° of roll—full left aileron, left rudder reapplied, slight back pressure beginning.
7. At 300–315° of roll—full left aileron, more left rudder, begin the increasing of back pressure. As the airplane approaches the wings-level attitude, the aileron, rudder, and elevator deflections are decreased as necessary to return to normal cruising flight (Fig. 4-2H).

Check the accelerometer after the roll is complete to see that approximately 2 g's were imposed on the initial pull-up (Fig. 4-3). (Again, this is for the C-150; about 2.5g's works best for the C-152.)

One of the problems with the first couple of aileron rolls is that when inverted you are so awed with your

Fig. 4-3. Accelerometer indications after a good aileron roll. You may prefer a slightly brisker (2.5-g) pull-up after you've done a few.

new position that you relax the aileron deflection, which of course slows down or stops any roll tendencies and you are left there (for a short while) to contemplate your shortcomings. The instructor will remind you to continue the roll. If you are inverted, *always roll* as a matter of recovery and never pull back on the control wheel or stick to do a half loop instead; it would take several hundred feet to recover, a decided disadvantage if you are on final approach when such trouble occurs.

Another problem you might have is neglecting to release back pressure when the airplane is inverted. The nose is allowed to drop and the airplane starts making knots earthward. Roll it out.

Fig. 4-4 gives an analysis of control positions for the aileron roll. Of course, you will be more interested in control *pressures,* but the instructor's drawing of this on the chalkboard and discussing it will help clear up any hazy areas about how the controls are used in an aileron roll to the left. Time zero of the illustration is when the airplane has reached the 30°-pitch position but no roll has started.

MORE ABOUT THE AILERON ROLL

Use of the Ailerons. Considering the aileron deflection throughout the roll (Fig. 4-4), it's usually best to move on in smoothly with full aileron deflection from the beginning, maintaining full deflection until the airplane approaches the normal wings-level attitude at the end of 360° of roll. The reason for this is to have a good rate of roll going from the beginning, to set up the impetus to get the airplane rolling so that the 360° is completed more quickly. Using 115 K (130 mph) as the entry speed, the speed at completion may be down to 80 K (90 mph). If the deflection is constant, as shown, the roll rate will be faster at first and will slow down as the speed decreases. The roll rate of a particular airplane is a function of aileron deflection and indicated (calibrated) airspeed (remember from Chap. 2, *control effectiveness = deflection × CAS*), and since the ailerons are already deflected fully, the roll rate must decrease with the airspeed.

A diagram of the roll rate of a particular airplane shows that it increases in a straight line with calibrated airspeed up to some point at which the dynamic pressure is too great for the pilot (or system) to maintain full aileron deflection, and then the roll rate decreases again (see Fig. 7-1).

Later, when you have the aileron roll pretty well in hand, the aileron deflection can start out at less than full and be increased as the airspeed decays to maintain a more-constant roll rate and smoother maneuver.

Use of the Rudder. Looking at the use of the rudder in the aileron roll (Fig. 4-4), you can see that as aileron is applied, rudder is also needed; since the maneuver is coordinated (if all goes well), the rudder is *always* applied in direction of roll, though to varying degrees.

Note that the rudder deflection curve has two peaks, *the second one higher than the first.* This is because the airspeed is decaying and the control effective-

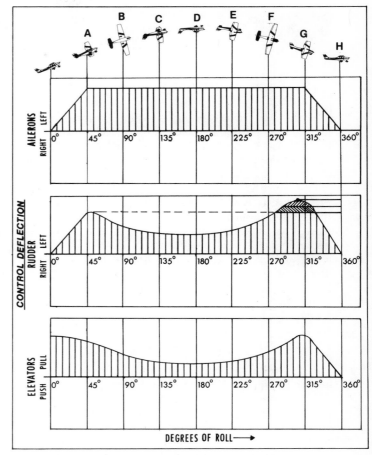

Fig. 4-4. Control deflections throughout a left aileron roll, starting at the 30°-nose-up attitude. Positions A–H here compare to A–H in Fig. 4-2.

ness is decreasing. Another factor, adverse yaw, which *increases* as the airspeed decreases, also requires more rudder because of the slower speed. The double problem of increased adverse yaw *and* less rudder effectiveness may require that nearly full rudder is needed for some airplanes at the second peak shown. At the end of 360° of roll, when the ailerons are neutralized, the rudder is no longer needed.

Improper *rudder* use in the aileron roll may cause problems that seem to come from poor elevator use. For instance, if the initial amount of rudder is held as the airplane passes the 45°- and approaches the 90°-roll position, the nose is pulled down and will be low at that point. The roll is completed in a nose-too-low position, with the elevator (or poor use of the elevator) as the apparent culprit.

If you note that the nose is high enough at the initiation of the roll and are relaxing the elevator pressure when inverted, do another roll and check the nose position at 90° of roll. Your rudder use may not have the "saddle" shown in Fig. 4-4. You may be thinking that poor elevator use is the culprit when rudder is really the problem. Many times you'll find that correcting the rudder problem is the item needed and your elevator pressures were fine all along.

Use of the Elevators. Note in Fig. 4-4 that the elevators are deflected up (you are "pulling") at the start of the roll, when the nose is at the 30°-nose-up position. As with the other controls, the line shows the relative positions of the elevators in the aileron roll. The elevators are never on the "down" side of the neutral position, and the g forces should always be positive. The back pressure is eased as the 90° position is passed, reaches its minimum at the inverted position (180° of roll), then is increased as necessary to bring the nose to the level flight position as the roll is completed. One g is pulled during the roll itself.

PRACTICING THE AILERON ROLL. When you are ready to start doing aileron rolls, your instructor will demonstrate one, explaining the maneuver. It may be that time and your ability will preclude the practice of more than a few aileron rolls the first flight, but if at all possible you should do at least one aileron roll yourself. After the demonstration, your instructor will review the actions in the maneuver (during a short rest period of straight and level flight), making sure that you understand that you must not neutralize the ailerons when the back pressure is relaxed as you approach the inverted position.

The follow-me-through method is normally a poor way to instruct flying, but in the aileron roll it is a good aid in getting the picture of control *movement,* and the instructor may have you do this. (You will work out the control pressures later yourself.) The first approach to some aerobatics *is* mechanical; natural feel will develop with practice. The main reason for the follow-me-through approach is to emphasize the necessity of relaxing that back pressure, *without* neutralizing the ailerons, as the airplane becomes inverted. The varying rudder action around the roll can also be felt.

You can figure that you are beginning to make real progress if you accidentally relax aileron pressure at some point in the roll and immediately correct it without any comment from the instructor.

Common Errors in the Aileron Roll

1. Not raising the nose high enough initially. This can carry on through the maneuver so that the nose is too low at the completion, even though the back pressure is relaxed the usual (or proper) amount. Following right along with this type of problem is a common tendency not to bring the nose up to the 30° attitude *fast enough.* You shouldn't yank the nose up abruptly; when the proper entry speed is reached, bring it up smoothly and fairly rapidly (otherwise, the speed decays before the roll is started).

If the airspeed is too low as you start the roll, stop the process and set it up again. If the airspeed is too low, the result will be a sloppy too-light-in-the-seat roll with a nose-low recovery (and a stall warning occurring as you try to pull the nose back up during the latter part of the roll).

2. Not coordinating aileron and rudder at the be-

Fig. 4-5. Slacking off of aileron deflection, too much back pressure at the last 90° of roll, *or* not enough rudder in the last 45° of roll can result in the nose being to the right of the reference at the completion of a left aileron roll.

ginning of the roll (the commonest error is not enough rudder).

3. Relaxing the aileron deflection as the airplane becomes inverted. (This happens pretty often at first.)

4. Neglecting to release enough back pressure when inverted. It will seem that you have to "shove forward," an unnatural action to the nonaerobatic pilot, and you will be uneasy about it at first. The *relaxation* of back pressure is not a sudden move as the airplane becomes inverted, but a subtle action that begins well before the 180°-roll position and continues well after that point. In a good aileron roll, the "passenger" should not be able to pinpoint the beginning or end of the relaxation of the back pressure. Back pressure and forward pressure can have a definite effect on heading control, particularly when the plane is vertically banked. After the instructor urges relaxing back pressure a few times, the deed is usually overdone. A relaxation that's too brisk or too soon can be felt as well as seen by the nose "oscillation" and heading error as the roll continues.

5. Not reapplying enough top rudder (left rudder in a left aileron roll) on the final part of the roll so that the airplane turns or dishes to one side. If in a left aileron roll the nose consistently ends up pointing to the right of reference, check for this, as well as too-soon or too-much relaxation of back pressure at the 90°-roll position. While this particular heading problem is being discussed, note that slacking off aileron pressure during the last 45–60° of roll can also result in an error in heading to the right (in a left roll) since the airplane tends to turn as the roll is delayed (Fig. 4-5). Reverse

the above directions for right roll problems. *Too much* back pressure during the last 45° of roll can also move the nose to the right of the reference.

6. Not applying enough back pressure in the last 45° of roll—allowing the nose to be too low. This, following an initially nose-low beginning, can result in a finale that is nose-low indeed.

7. Ending the roll with the bank 10–15° short of completion.

The right aileron roll in the Aerobat is more difficult for the average pilot. Since traffic patterns are predominantly left-hand and other training procedures seem to favor turns (and rolls) to the left, most people have a stronger tendency to neutralize the ailerons and let the nose drop in a right roll. You might also note that more rudder is needed all the way around (U.S. airplanes). Because of this, more heading problems may be encountered in the right roll. However, some pilots start out with better right rolls than with left ones.

AND MORE PRACTICE OF THE AILERON ROLL. You won't beat aileron rolls to death before moving on to the loop. Even if your rolls aren't "quite" perfect, the instructor will move on to loops, and then *loops followed by rolls.* These latter rolls will be better as you set up a rhythm doing the combination and start doing the rolls without conscious effort. This is not to say that you won't continue to work on your aileron rolls

throughout your aerobatic career, but it's been found that too-long and too-concentrated attention to one maneuver can result in decreasing performance as you get fixated on minor details.

Later, you won't pull the nose up so high as 30° when initiating the aileron roll but will tighten up the helix. You'll see that a good smooth roll can be done with an initial pull-up attitude of 15-20°. The 30°-pitch attitude is done at first to allow you time to complete the 360° roll without ending up with a nose-low attitude.

THE LOOP

The loop is considered one of the simplest maneuvers to do, but to do it well requires more planning and coordination than is apparent at first. The loop is basically a 360° "turn" in a vertical plane (Fig. 4-6). You may have heard from your experimenting, non-aerobatic pilot friends that "all I do is dive to a high speed and keep pulling back on the wheel"—*not true.* You need to know the *correct* procedure. This maneuver is the one in which you will encounter the effects of 3 g's or more for the first time, and it's likely that the instructor will handle the throttle for your first few loops, since the average aerobatic trainee has trouble coordinating throttle and elevators at first.

"So the loop is a 360° in a vertical plane"—the

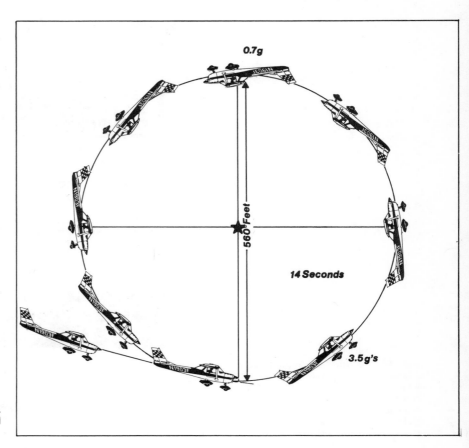

Fig. 4-6. General look at the loop in the Aerobat. Fourteen seconds is an average time from initial pull-up back to level flight attitude.

maneuver is so well known that a description of *what* it is usually is unnecessary, but you might use the model to get an overall look at it. Usually, the loop is not demonstrated until the second flight; however, if you are an extra-sharp person who's been doing very well at aileron rolls, you may start earlier.

The loop, one of the fundamental maneuvers of aerobatic flight, should be practiced not only to learn to do it properly but also to smooth it out as a part of more advanced maneuvers. After practicing a number of loops, you'll notice that your orientation has improved radically. It's also good for getting the feel of the elevator pressures with changes in airspeed.

PROCEDURE IN THE LOOP. Everybody, student pilot to ATPC pilot, knows "how to do a loop," as mentioned earlier. They think it's simply a maneuver that requires a lot of "pull." This may also be your attitude—at first. Following are the steps in the loop (illustrated by Fig. 4-7, points *A–J*).

Line the airplane up directly over a long, straight stretch of road or railroad. Clear the area and ease the nose over to pick up an entry speed of 120 K (140 mph) (point *A*). Continue to watch for other airplanes as the entry speed is approached (point *B*). Throttle back as necessary to keep from exceeding the rpm red line. As the recommended speed is reached, initiate a smooth pull-up (point *C*). Ease the throttle to full-open as the nose approaches vertical, making sure that no engine overspeeding occurs.

Use the left wing tip as a reference to check after the horizon disappears under the nose; looking over the nose would only show blue sky (or clouds) through nearly all the top 180° of the loop, which makes orientation difficult (points *D–F*). The accelerometer should be indicating +3.5 g's (but don't stare at it). Open the throttle fully at point *E*.

As the airplane nose passes the vertical, the airspeed will continue to be decreasing rapidly and more up-elevator deflection will be needed (the control *pres-*

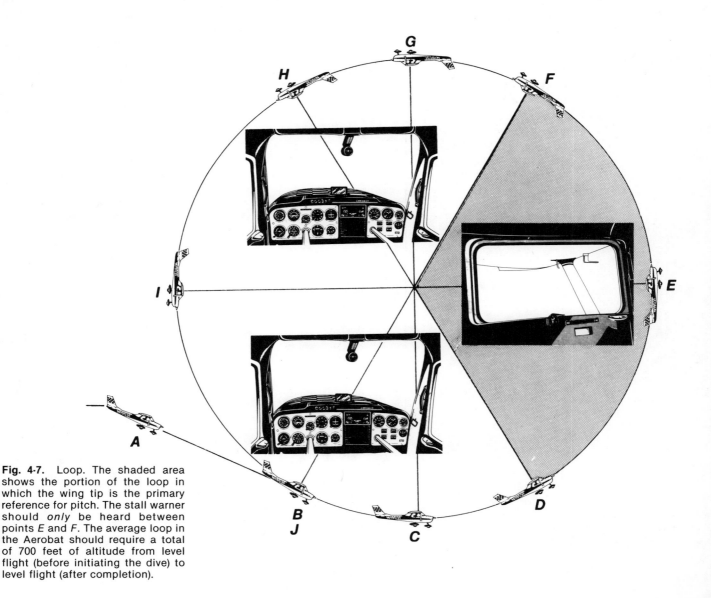

Fig. 4-7. Loop. The shaded area shows the portion of the loop in which the wing tip is the primary reference for pitch. The stall warner should *only* be heard between points *E* and *F*. The average loop in the Aerobat should require a total of 700 feet of altitude from level flight (before initiating the dive) to level flight (after completion).

sures will be getting lighter).

As the airplane approaches the inverted attitude (when the nose is an estimated 30° above the horizon), relax the back pressure slightly to avoid buffeting and to maintain a more symmetrical pattern (point *F*). Some loops look like a handwritten *e* because pilots neglect this. Keep the back pressure relaxed until the nose has passed below the horizon on the back side of the loop (about 30° down). As the inverted position is reached, check that the wings are level with the horizon (point *G*). Increase the back pressure gradually during the final part of the dive recovery (point *H*). (Don't be too hasty or a stall will result.) A proper pull-up at the beginning of the loop will probably result in about a +3.5-g indication on the accelerometer.

Retard the throttle as the airplane approaches the vertical (nose-down) attitude on the back side of the loop (Fig. 4-7*I*) so that the engine limits are not exceeded, but don't close the throttle because at high speeds engine-prop roughness could occur. Be sure the wings are exactly perpendicular to the road, railroad, or section line reference.

The final part of the loop will probably result in an accelerometer reading of about +3.0 g's (point *J*), and the airspeed will be at or slightly below the entry speed. (Again, *don't* stare at the accelerometer as an indicator during the initial pull-up; use it as a check afterward.)

Recover to level cruising flight. From point *C* to point *C* again (Fig. 4-7) should take about 14 seconds.

Fig. 4-8A–J reviews the steps in the loop. Compare them with points *A–J* in Fig. 4-7.

You should have positive-g forces acting on you all the way around the loop; the forces will be less at the top of the loop than during the pull-up and recovery, but the occupants should be comfortable (no hanging in the belt and harness). You both may feel a little light in your seat on one or two of your first loops but should be able to work it out without much trouble.

The arrows in Fig. 4-9 show the relative amount of g's and back pressure being applied around the loop. For this example, the recommended entry speed is 120 K, and the minimum speed at the top of the loop is 60 K, one-half the maximum. (It is assumed that +1 g is being pulled at the top and that the loop is perfectly symmetrical, that is, that the radius is the same all the way around—this can be easily done on paper, anyway. Assume these are "net" g's.)

The lower part of this "ideally symmetrical loop"

Fig. 4-8A–J. Steps in the loop, as seen from the cockpit and alongside the airplane.

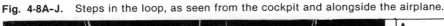

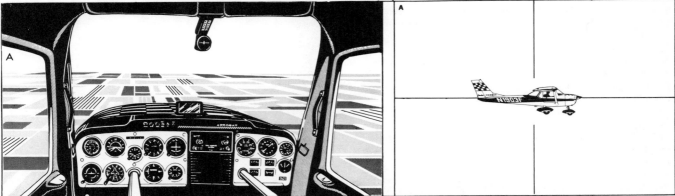

(A) Clear the area before starting the loop, *then* ease the nose over (wings level).

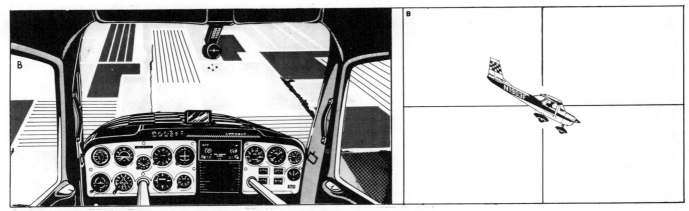

(B) Here the airplane is at the recommended entry speed (120 K for the Aerobat).

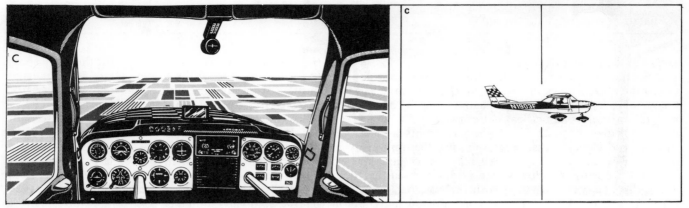

(C) The pull-up has started and the airplane is passing through the level-pitch attitude.

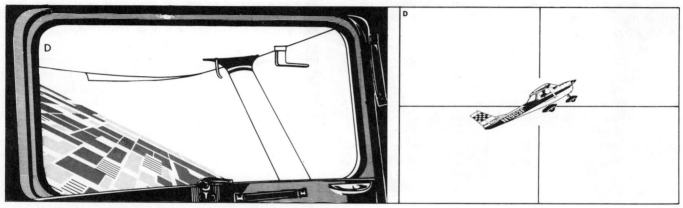

(D) At this point 3.5 g's are being pulled. Start looking at the wing tip.

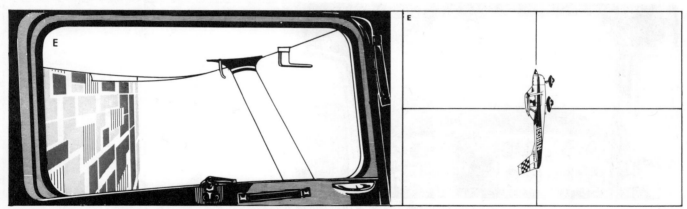

(E) The pitch attitude is vertical. Check the wing tip reference on the horizon and open the throttle fully. The stall warner will start sounding at this point.

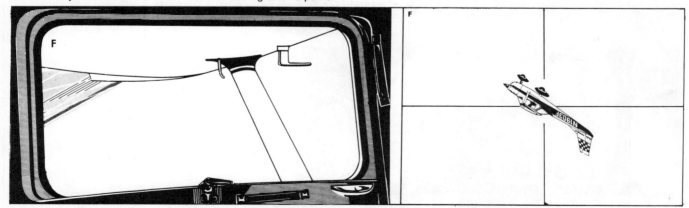

(F) At this point (nose 30° above the horizon), relax the back pressure just enough to silence the stall warner and move your view back from the wing to the nose (and through the skylights in the Aerobat).

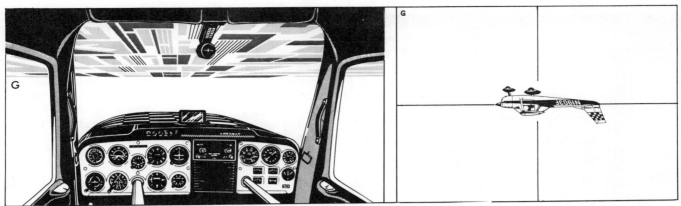

(G) Still relax back pressure slightly. Check that the wings are level in reference to the horizon.

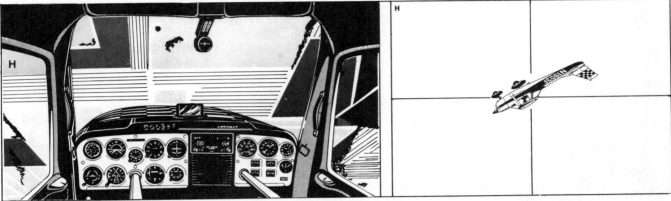

(H) At this point (nose 30° below the horizon), start smoothly reapplying back pressure.

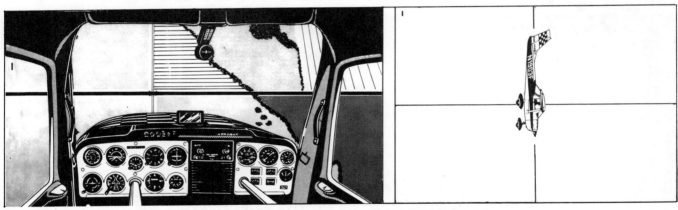

(I) As the pitch attitude reaches vertical, reduce power and make sure that the wings are perpendicular to the reference line (the light-colored road, here). Continue the back pressure. (Some pilots subconsciously believe that the airplane can't be stalled with the nose straight down and are able to do interesting maneuvers when the back pressure is applied too enthusiastically.)

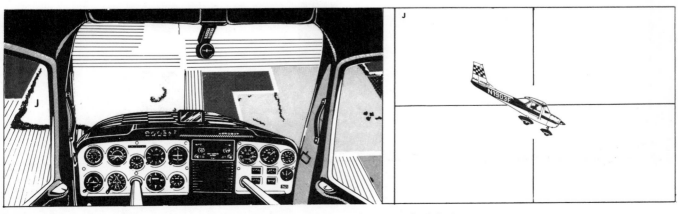

(J) Continue the pull-out. The airplane will be pulling about 3.0 g's, and you may feel the bump at this point.

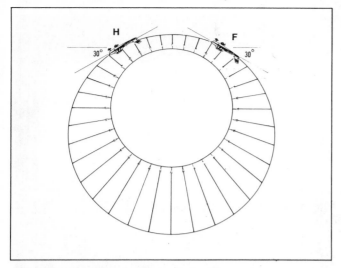

Fig. 4-9. Relative amount of "pull" required around a loop.

Fig. 4-10. Accelerometer readings after a loop in the Aerobat.

should have the same radius as the +1-g top, as an interesting point comes to light: The centrifugal force in a constant-radius turn (or loop) is a function of the square of the airspeed. If you double the airspeed, the g forces required to maintain that same radius will be *4* times that found at the lower speed. So, in this theoretical approach, a maximum of +4 g's is needed at the bottom of the loop to maintain 1 g at the top. It's complicated slightly in the practical application by, for example, the change in power used during the loop, so that a pull-up of +3.5 g's may be the maximum required.

The rate of "pull" varies, as shown by the arrows in Fig. 4-9, but things aren't as neat and predictable as that. There are other factors involved, not the least of which is that it is not humanly possible to vary the back pressure so precisely, so a more mechanical procedure is used, as shown by points *F* and *H* in Figs. 4-7, 4-8, and 4-9. At point *F* the nose is at 30° above the horizon and the back pressure is relaxed. At point *H*, 30° below the horizon, the back pressure is started again and gradually increased.

One indication of a good loop is that the altitude at the bottom (level flight) is the same as the altitude at the initial pull-up.

A somewhat mechanical aid for the Aerobat is that

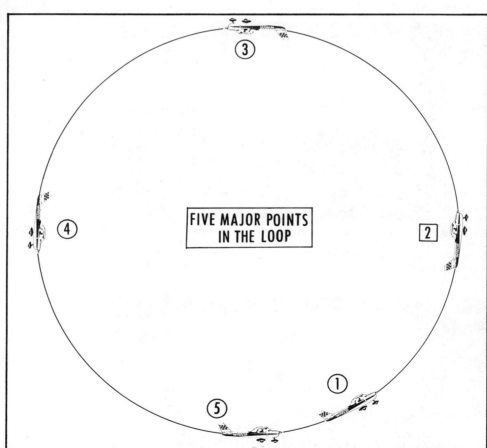

FIVE MAJOR POINTS
IN THE LOOP

Fig. 4-11. Five points for checking wing attitude during the loop.

the stall warner will be sounding as you are pulling through from the vertical pitch. At the 30°-nose-up position (point *F*), relax just enough back pressure to silence it. This works well for early loop practice.

A good initial all-around check for a good loop in the Aerobat is a +3.5-g pull-up and about +0.7 g at the top. This gives a steady, not-too-light-in-the-seat maneuver (Fig. 4-10). Your instructor will check the active hand of the accelerometer at the pull-up and at the top of the loop during your efforts.

MORE ABOUT THE LOOP

Wing Attitude. There are five major points for checking the wing attitude in doing the loop (Fig. 4-11). At point *1* the wings should be level, although some rugged individualists are already well banked by this time.

Usually the problem of wing attitude starts between points *1* and *2*. You are "pulling," and probably a banking force is being exerted on the control wheel as well.

The wing attitude should be noted at point *2*, but it will take experience to tell whether a wing is "down" or not (Fig. 4-12).

It's pretty easy to see where you stand at point *3* of Fig. 4-11, because the horizon is a good reference. A correction should be made there if necessary. You will consider it very difficult to understand *which way* to roll to correct for a wing-down problem there, but you'll do what comes naturally when it's required. This is a good place to remember that the airplane flies relative to *you* when the controls are deflected, regardless of its flight attitude.

Checking the wing attitude at point *4* of Fig. 4-11 is easy because the airplane will be pointing straight down at the prechosen road. (If possible, always line up over a long straight stretch of road for practicing loops, Cuban eights, and cloverleafs.) The power should be reduced at this point.

When the airplane is at point *5* of Fig. 4-11, it's a little late to save the maneuver, but you still should check it because it's good for air discipline, and if the loop is to be followed by another maneuver (particularly another loop), the proper wing attitude should be looked at here.

Look back at Fig. 4-7. By looking at the wing tip between points *D* and *F* (the shaded area), you will be able to maintain a nearly constant pitch change. Some people pull up just fine at point *D* but slack off back pressure as the nose passes vertically (between points *E* and *F*), and the airplane doesn't continue the prescribed path. The result is a condition that is too slow and sloppy over the top, with people tending to float out of their seats—and the microphone out of its clip, weaving "up" in front of the instrument panel like a mesmerized cobra.

Bumps. Your instructor will indicate that you may feel a "bump" in the loop and other maneuvers if the airplane

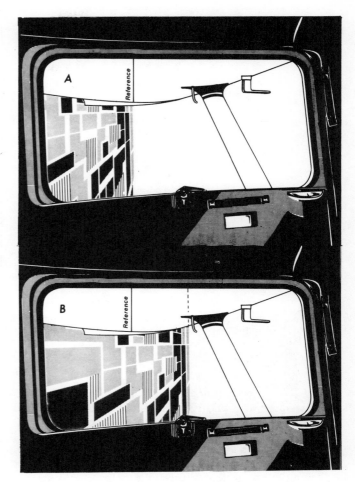

Fig. 4-12. Checking the wing attitude at the vertical pitch-up attitude. **(A)** The proper wing position. **(B)** The wing is low, either because of an input of left aileron during the initial pull-up or lack of "torque" correction as the airspeed decays (at full power). **(C)** Some few people have a "high" wing at this point, caused by input of *right* aileron during the pull-up.

stays within the original vertical plane of flight (you're hitting your own wake turbulence). Some instructors advocate a very short period of straight and level flight before the loop pull-up while others may prefer a direct pull-up from the shallow dive as the recommended entry speed is reached. The initial pull-up point will have a bearing as to where you feel the bump (Fig. 4-13). Some of the good, solid bumps can be quite startling if you haven't been warned about them. The initial thought is that you probably pulled too hard in the loop and some major component(s) has departed the airplane.

Use of the Rudder. Rudder use, like wing attitude, won't be covered by the instructor in much detail at first, but later, when you have a good grasp of elevator handling, the proper use of the rudder in the loop should be introduced. Rudder use has a lot to do with wing attitude since yaw can induce roll problems. Basi-

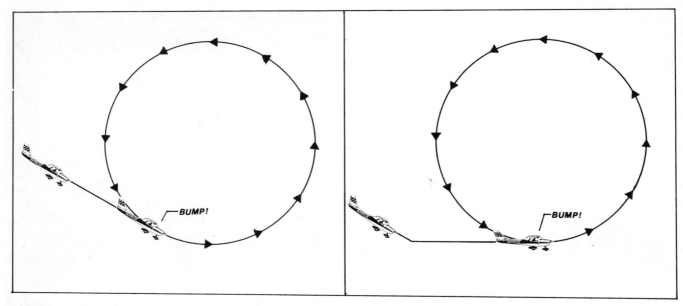

Fig. 4-13. Some instructors prefer to start the loop from a dive, while others prefer a short period of level flight before the pull-up. The selected procedure establishes where the bump will be felt.

cally, for most U.S. airplanes left rudder is needed in a higher-speed dive and right rudder is needed in a climb and at any low speeds with high power settings.

Common Errors in the Loop

1. Neglecting to keep an eye on the tachometer during the initial dive—exceeding the engine limits.

2. Making the initial pull-up too easy—the airplane is too slow as the top of the loop is approached. (It is possible to decrease speed too rapidly by too much pressure as well, but a too-easy pull-up is one of the commoner errors.) Even if the proper initial amount of back pressure is used, there is a tendency to slack off in the second 90° of the loop, allowing the pitch change rate to decrease, and the airplane gets sloppy on top as noted earlier.

3. Applying initial back pressure too abruptly or too jerkily. This problem may arise as you do more loops. It is usually an overreaction to earlier timidity at this point in the maneuver. The back pressure should be enough to do the job and applied smoothly.

4. Inadvertently applying aileron as back pressure is being exerted on the pull-up, so the lateral axis does not stay parallel to the horizon—the airplane is *banked*. In the inverted position the wings should be parallel to the horizon. Later you'll be able to correct for any deviations handily. Again, indication of good control of wing attitude is encountering your own wake turbulence as the loop is completed.

5. Neglecting to relax the back pressure as the inverted position is being approached, so the airplane makes a tight rotation at the top—with buffeting and a possible stall. One reason for this is that right after the +3.5 g pull-up, +0.7 g may seem too light so you

subconsciously try to keep up the g forces.

6. Relaxing back pressures too positively—the occupants may tend to hang in the belt and harness. This is usually an overcompensation for common error 5.

7. Forgetting to retard the throttle in the last part of the loop—exceeding the engine rpm limits.

8. Applying too-abrupt back pressure on the back side of the loop so that buffeting or a stall occurs. This usually occurs between points *3* and *4* in Fig. 4-11.

9. If there is a strong crosswind at your altitude the loop may drift slightly away from the road during the 20 seconds or so required to complete the full maneuver (dive plus loop). You may try to "point" the airplane over to the road during the last 90° of the circle, changing or bending the plane of the loop instead of paralleling the road. If it appears that crosswind is a real problem, you'd better pick a road parallel with the wind, or do the loops perpendicular to the original road.

AND MORE PRACTICE OF THE LOOP. After you have had practice with the loop and can do the maneuver reasonably well, the instructor will let you handle the throttle. Expect a slight deterioration in performance when you start this. Usually the problem is that you are so carefully watching the tachometer that you prematurely relax the back pressure as the nose is pointing straight up, which makes for a certain looseness and poor path control at the top of the loop.

This brings up the question, Should you use both hands on the wheel in the loop? An advantage of using both hands is that the back pressure on the wheel will be more symmetrical, with less of a tendency to introduce aileron deflections during the maneuver (and for smaller people two hands are virtually required during the first few loops practiced in certain airplanes). If possible however, use the one-hand-on-the-wheel, one-hand-on-the-throttle procedure, because when two hands are used on the pull-up a change in back pressure results as one hand is taken from the wheel to add power and then returned to the wheel. There may be a slight change, as well, as power is reduced on the back side of the loop.

After a dozen or so loops (not in a row!) you should be able to complete the maneuver, recognizing

Fig. 4-14. Accelerometer indications after a more symmetrical loop.

and correcting for elevator and aileron use errors. You might expect an occasional feeling of being "slightly light" at the inverted position, but after a dozen loops you should be able to see your mistakes and start analyzing each one yourself. The instructor will make sure that you are able to do the basic loop well before moving on to the cloverleaf, Cuban eight, and Immelmann since these maneuvers are more complicated variations of it.

Later you'll want to ensure that the loop is symmet-

rical and may use a slightly higher g pull-up initially and more-relaxed back pressure at the top so that the airplane "floats" across. This looks better from the ground than the earlier combination of +3.5 and +0.7 g's; a good final reading for this is the +4.0- and 0-g accelerometer indication shown in Fig. 4-14.

THE SNAP ROLL

The snap roll, the third of the Three Fundamentals, is often described as a "horizontal spin," which is exactly what it is, if you realize that entry is that of a very accelerated spin entry with +2.5 to +3.0 g's occurring at the instant of stall break. It's sort of like a movie of a normal 1-g spin entry speeded up a couple of times.

The snap roll is basically a timing maneuver and a good aid in developing orientation ability. The coordination of rudder and elevator (and ailerons in some airplanes) that is required is not the type of coordination encountered in normal flight.

Okay, so the snap roll is a spin done in a horizontal direction (Fig. 4-15). The airplane is stalled at a higher-than-normal speed, and an imbalance of lift is created when the rudder is fully deflected as the stall is introduced. The result is an accelerated stall with a rapid rotation in the direction of the applied rudder. To recover, use the same technique as for the spin recovery—opposite rudder and smooth yet positive, firm forward movement of the control wheel. The opposite rudder and the forward movement of the wheel stop the rotation and break the stall. If timed properly (starting about three-fourths of the way around), the recovery should be to wings-level flight at a speed 15–20 K below the entry speed.

The true snap roll is considered to be a maneuver using only the rudder and elevator, but for the Aerobat (and some other airplanes), aileron is used in the direc-

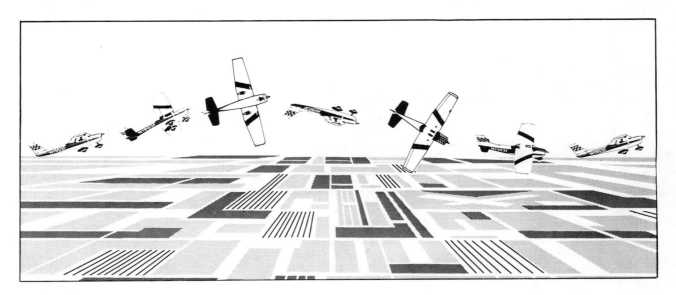

Fig. 4-15. Snap roll, a side view.

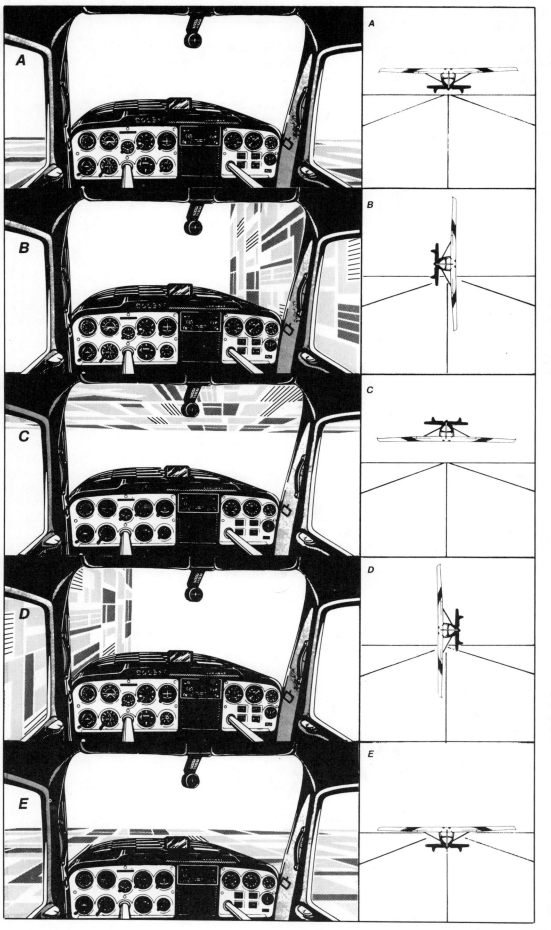

Fig. 4-16A–E. Right snap roll as seen from the cockpit and from behind the airplane.

(A) The airplane is at the recommended snap roll airspeed (80 K for the Aerobat) with full power, the pitch attitude slightly nose-up.

(B) Full right rudder and full aft wheel have been applied. After rotation has started, full right aileron is added.

(C) Right rudder, aft wheel, and right aileron are still held.

(D) At the 270° position, opposite (left) rudder and aileron are applied and the wheel moved smoothly forward.

(E) When the rotation has stopped, the controls are neutralized and normal cruise resumes.

tion of roll to help *after* the rotation gets started (opposite aileron also can be an aid in making precise recoveries). You'll soon be automatically using the ailerons as necessary to help start and stop the maneuver.

PROCEDURE IN THE SNAP ROLL. Fig. 4-16A–E shows a right snap roll in sequence from the cockpit and from behind the airplane.

Ease the airplane's nose up from level flight to shallow climb at the recommended speed of 80 K (90 mph), using full power. You'll do better to attain 85 K, *then* ease the nose up so that the airplane's nose will hit the climb attitude just as 80 K is reached (Fig. 4-16A). This stops a tendency to be nose-low as the snap roll is completed. Smoothly and quickly pull the control wheel (or stick) straight back to the full-aft position while simultaneously applying full rudder in the desired direction of roll (Fig. 4-16B). In the Aerobat, as soon as the stall breaks and rotation starts, apply full aileron in the direction of roll. Keep full rudder, elevator, and aileron deflected. Don't use aileron until the rotation set up by the rudder-elevator combination has started. Premature use of aileron tends to "unstall" that inside wing, and little or no rotation will occur—the Aerobat will buffet and wallow, and you'll have to neutralize the controls and start all over again.

At about three-fourths of the roll completion (270° of rotation), apply opposite rudder and aileron and move the control wheel forward to break the stall (Fig. 4-16D). When the rotation has stopped, neutralize the controls and assume normal cruise. The chances are good that the recovery from your first few snap rolls with not be in *exact* wings-level flight; you may need to do several before attaining the ability to stay oriented.

The first time a snap roll is demonstrated by the instructor, the maneuver will likely be completed before you realize it has started. Later you'll be surprised at how the action seems to slow down; orientation will be no problem and the snap roll will no longer be a blur of ground, horizon, and sky gyrating in (apparently) all directions.

Here's the point where time becomes an obvious factor in g-force effects. Even though you'll pull up to 3 g's, about the same as in parts of a loop, the time factor makes them seem much less. The average aerobatic trainee who is asked after that first loop to estimate how many g's were pulled will say, "About 12, I reckon." After a snap roll, the estimate will probably be 1½ g's (a slight exaggeration, and it's not the g force that could cause queasiness in the snap but the "uncoordinated rolling").

Common Errors in the Snap Roll

1. Not moving the control wheel or stick aft fast enough—the "snap" is more of a "mush."

2. Trying to use the ailerons instead of the rudder to get rotation started. This is particularly evident after you've been doing a number of aileron rolls.

3. Not enough rudder or elevator deflection at the initiation so that the airplane is in a slow, yawing, non-stalled roll.

4. Neglecting to add ailerons after the roll has started (Aerobat).

5. Having poor timing on recovery. Expect that you will overshoot the stopping point on the first few recoveries. Later, for a change of pace, you'll probably start the recovery too soon but will get the corrected timing after a few more snaps. If you find yourself inverted from an accidental half snap or snap and one-half, remember to *roll* out.

6. Shoving the wheel or stick forward on the recovery—making the occupants feel light on the seat, pushing the nose well down below the horizon, and emptying the ashtrays. Although positive forward pressure is necessary, it can be overdone. Usually the problem is that the forward pressure is held after the recovery has been effected. You will find after practice in the Aerobat that you can start earlier, moving the wheel forward slowly, and control the stopping point (wings level) much better than trying to time an abrupt wheel-forward movement.

7. *Not* moving the wheel or stick forward after applying opposite rudder and aileron—the stall is not broken and the airplane may rotate or snap back to a banked attitude with the nose down (and with a lot of buffeting and wallowing). You may not realize that you're holding the back pressure and wonder why the airplane apparently has a mind of its own.

SUMMARY

Get these Three Fundamentals well in hand and you can move on to the combinations and more complicated maneuvers you've been wanting to do.

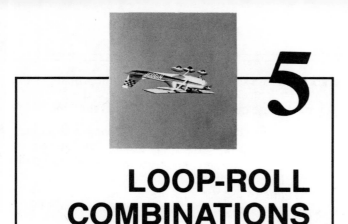

5

LOOP-ROLL COMBINATIONS

LOOPS FOLLOWED BY AILERON ROLLS

In Chap. 4, in covering the aileron roll, it was mentioned that after a reasonable period of practice you'll move on to the loop, and then the loop followed by an aileron roll (Fig. 5-1). You'll do a loop (the instructor may handle the throttle again for the first loop-roll combination) and at the bottom of the loop you'll ease the nose up to the 30°-pitch attitude and do an aileron roll. You should alternate the direction of roll with subsequent loops. (The tendency is to roll in that one direction you like best.) You'll find here, too, that you can, with practice, tighten up these aileron rolls (an initial pitch-up of 15–20°) as you get more proficient.

Since you've reduced power on the backside of the loop, it's a good idea to move in with full power for the roll to keep any altitude loss to a minimum. However, open the throttle *after* the airplane is inverted; this will allow the airspeed to be low enough so that prop overspeeding won't occur. You'll wonder at first how you can be rolling the airplane and use power too, but if it's done as—or just after—you become inverted you won't have to worry about looking at the tach to check for overspeed.

As noted earlier, you'll find that your aileron rolls will improve when done immediately following a loop. Also, most people really enjoy the combination as this seems to be "real aerobatics" at last. It's a good feeling to line up directly over a road or railroad, do the loop and roll, and see that the airplane is still lined up with it as the wings are level again.

Common Errors in the Loop–Aileron Roll Combination

1. Any of the errors discussed in Chap. 4 for the separate loop and aileron roll. (Check those common errors for each maneuver now, while you're thinking about it.)

2. Thinking about errors in the loop when you are already in the aileron roll. Usually, doing this ensures enough distraction in the aileron roll that after it's complete you can worry about roll errors *as well as* loop errors. Once a portion of a maneuver or series of maneuvers is complete, concentrate on the item you are doing *now*. You can analyze any problems immediately after the maneuver or series is complete and then do a more complete review after you get on the ground.

3. Pulling the nose too high when coming out of the loop and initiating the roll (some people really get into the spirit of the thing and apparently are already thinking about another loop). The best thing in this case is to continue the loop if you are already approaching a vertical pitch and have started close to the proper loop speed. This is better on you *and* the airplane than a vertical roll. Your instructor may discuss a hammerhead stall as a method of recovery from such a deteriorating situation. The hammerhead stall or turn can be discussed in a general way, but *the hammerhead is not an approved maneuver for the Aerobat.*

4. Keeping the nose too low (level or lower) as the roll is started so that the aileron roll ends up as a nose-low, high-g, altitude-losing maneuver.

5. Not completing the roll. Some aerobatic train-

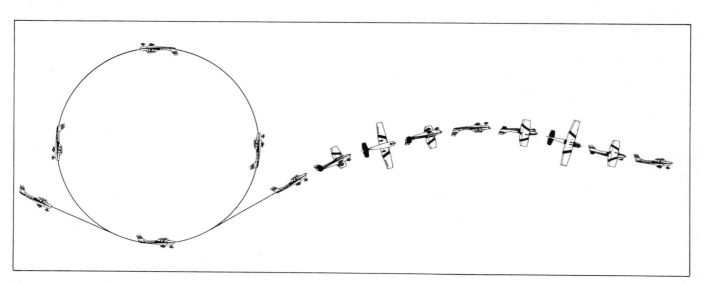

Fig. 5-1. Loop followed by an aileron roll.

ees are particularly prone, in the aileron roll following the loop, to stop the roll about 10–15° bank shy of completion, while congratulating themselves on a job well done.

THE CLOVERLEAF—A LOOP WITH A QUARTER-ROLL RECOVERY

The maneuvers most commonly flown using a combination of the loop and roll are the *cloverleaf, Cuban eight,* and *Immelmann.* The cloverleaf is four loops each with a *quarter-roll recovery* (the four quarter rolls are made in the same direction). When seen obliquely, the path of the plane traces the outline of a four-leaf clover. The rolls are done as the airplane reaches the vertical nose-down attitude (Fig. 5-2).

The cloverleaf, disregarding the physical effort involved, is the easiest of the three loop-roll maneuvers because the airplane is pointed straight down and the airspeed is picking up, making the controls more effective, and because the references for the 90° (quarter) roll are readily seen. The Cuban eight and Immelmann (both of which require a *half roll* at a lower airspeed) are more difficult, in the order mentioned, for the new

aerobatic pilot—particularly in a lower-powered aerobatic airplane. (These maneuvers will be discussed later.)

Your instructor will introduce the loop with a quarter-roll recovery, probably doing only one or two at first. After you are able to make the 90° roll and pull-up to level flight, your instructor will bring in the idea of combining two, then three, and finally four to complete a cloverleaf. Doing the full cloverleaf can be physically tiring, so the instructor may have you stick to a maximum of two loops with quarter rolls until later in the training.

The cloverleaf is hard to draw on a chalkboard since it's a three-dimensional maneuver, but the instructor can make it clear by using a model airplane. You may be asked to take the model and demonstrate it to check on your knowledge of what you are expected to do.

Although it looks complicated, the loop with a quarter-roll recovery is no more than a combination of two of the Three Fundamentals, which you can now do individually—or at least you *should* be able to do them before you start on this maneuver.

One of the problems you might have is the tend-

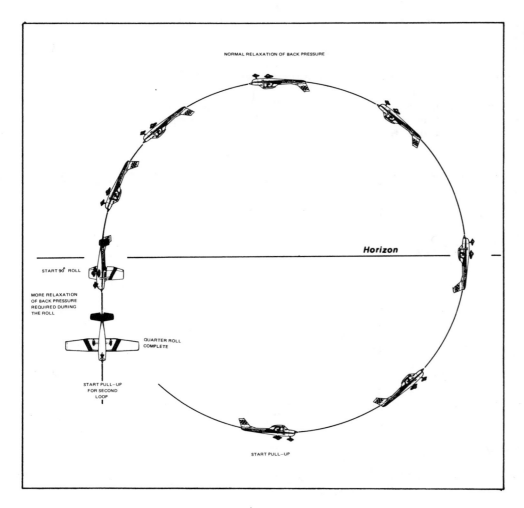

Fig. 5-2. Loop with a quarter-roll recovery (one-fourth of a cloverleaf).

ency to let the nose come up during the quarter roll, which results in the airspeed being too low for another loop. When you practice a single loop and quarter roll, make sure that you complete it with enough speed to enter another loop if desired, or you'll start a habit that will follow over to the full cloverleaf.

To repeat, the instructor will demonstrate the loop and quarter-roll recovery and may do two parts of it but normally won't do the full cloverleaf if you seem to have the idea. The instructor will likely handle the throttle for your first cloverleaf or two.

PROCEDURE IN THE CLOVERLEAF. It's best to line up directly over a road, railroad, or section line, so that the loop portion can be checked. As for the roll portion, you don't have to be directly over a road to judge a 90° roll; you can estimate the roll very well from a parallel position.

The first few times you will tend to bring the nose up as soon as the roll is completed, and it will take a definite effort on your part to keep the nose down and attain the airspeed for the next loop.

Lead the next loop entry speed by about 10 K for the Aerobat, since the nose is—or should be—pointed straight down as the quarter roll is completed. (For the Cuban eight, where the nose is pointed down at a 45° angle when the half roll is completed, a lead of 5 K on pull-up is recommended.) Of course, speaking generally, you will work out the best lead for your particular type of airplane and maneuver. Fig. 5-3 shows an example for the Aerobat.

After the instructor has admonished you a few times about your too-early (low-speed) pull-up in the cloverleaf, you'll find that you may start letting the speed build up so high that the altitude loss at the completion of even one loop is unacceptable. Watch for this.

The quarter roll should be "brisk," not dragged out; this means good use of rudder. The fairly rapid roll makes the maneuver easier to do because after you complete the roll you are free to concentrate on the airspeed and pitch attitude.

Fig. 5-4A-C shows a view from the cockpit at the start, 45°-roll position, and completion of a quarter roll to the left.

The cloverleaf is the logical first real combination of the loop and roll to be introduced, for three primary reasons:

1. The airplane is pointed straight down and even people who tend to stare over the nose in *every* aerobatic maneuver can hardly fail to see that reference road or railroad rushing up at them. In other words, you're pointed right at your reference and have the best view of it.

2. Since the airplane is pointed straight down, the airspeed is picking up about as rapidly as possible, and you remember from earlier in this book that *control effectiveness = deflection × CAS,* so that the controls are quickly becoming effective (from the slow speed at the top of the loop).

3. Only a quarter roll (90°) is required, although for some this might be more difficult than a half (180°) or full (360°) roll, since the starting and stopping actions are relatively close together.

Common Errors in the Cloverleaf

1. Not concentrating on each part of the loop or roll—thinking about the roll while doing the loop, or vice versa.

2. Pulling the nose up too soon after the quarter roll is completed—the airspeed is too low for the next loop.

3. Failing to check the wing tip at the proper sec-

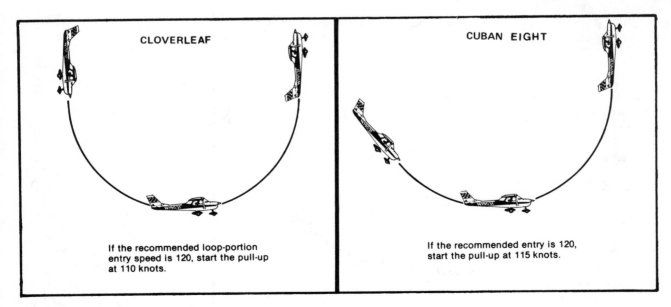

CLOVERLEAF

CUBAN EIGHT

If the recommended loop-portion entry speed is 120, start the pull-up at 110 knots.

If the recommended entry is 120, start the pull-up at 115 knots.

Fig. 5-3.   Suggested airspeed leads for the Aerobat. (From *The Flight Instructor's Manual*)

Fig. 5-4A–C. Vertical quarter roll to the left.

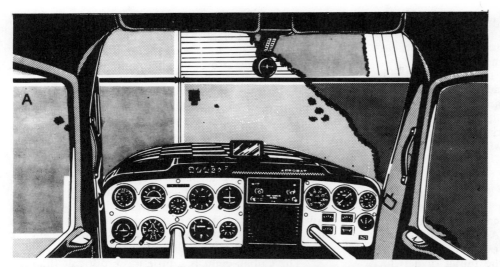

(A) A brisk roll is started as the nose reaches the vertical (down) position.

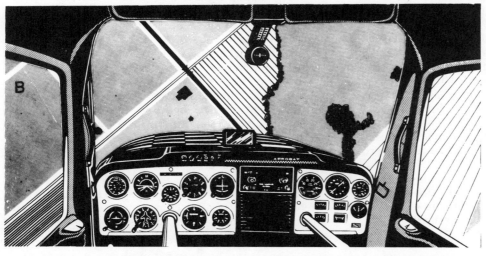

(B) Use sufficient rudder with the aileron so that the roll is "brisk" but coordinated. The 45° of roll position is shown here.

(C) The quarter roll is complete and the pull-up just starting.

tions of the loop—reverting back to the habit of staring over the nose.

4. Keeping the nose down too long on the back side of the loop—losing too much altitude.

5. Making a too-slow quarter roll, usually the result of not enough rudder with the aileron.

6. Handling the throttle poorly—applying power too soon and/or retarding it too late.

7. Pulling back on the wheel asymmetrically—the loops aren't completed with the wings perpendicular or parallel to the road.

PRACTICING THE CLOVERLEAF. The average trainee usually tends to let the airspeed get higher with each loop portion of a cloverleaf. You can figure that you are proceeding very well if with the Aerobat you only lose 100 ft for each additional loop portion of the cloverleaf, or 300 ft in addition to the initial dive (which might take about 700 ft). Your instructor will know the average for any particular type of airplane you are using and use this as an evaluation of your progress in the loop-type maneuvers. The accelerometer will indicate approximately the same as for the single loop.

Keep checking the loop portion of this maneuver (the average person tends to get a little sloppy in this portion while practicing more and more cloverleafs and getting involved in the whole maneuver). The instructor may have to remind you that you must concentrate on each part, but don't dwell on one part while going on to the next.

You may get some pretty hefty "bumps" in the cloverleaf (usually when headed straight down in the last three loops). Don't worry—congratulate yourself if you get three good bumps in a full cloverleaf.

THE CUBAN EIGHT

The Cuban eight is also a maneuver that combines parts of the loop and the aileron roll. The airplane's path describes a figure eight lying on its side (Fig. 5-5). Basically, it is three-fourths of a loop and a descending half aileron roll (180°) with the nose down at an angle of approximately 45° when the half roll is completed to "right-side-up" flight. The nose is kept down at the 45° angle until the recommended entry speed is again attained (assuming a proper airspeed lead); then the second loop portion of the maneuver is started. When the airplane is again inverted with the nose down at about a 30° angle, the half aileron roll is completed again to an upright attitude (45° pitch down). Cruising flight is regained after the second loop and half roll. The Cuban eight is easily drawn on the board, but a model is the greatest aid.

The Cuban eight is a little more difficult than the cloverleaf because the pitch attitude at the roll is not straight down. This means (1) the reference is a little harder to see, (2) the airspeed (and control effectiveness) is not picking up quite so fast, and (3) 90° more roll is required.

This maneuver is one of the best for getting you involved in aerobatics. You've seen the Cuban eight at airshows and competitions, and this one grabs your attention. The cloverleaf, although a fairly complex maneuver, is basically four loops in succession, whereas the Cuban eight appears to be a *real* exercise in precision (which, of course, it is).

PRACTICING THE CUBAN EIGHT. The instructor will review the loop briefly, citing such points as throttle handling, where to look, and points of relaxation of

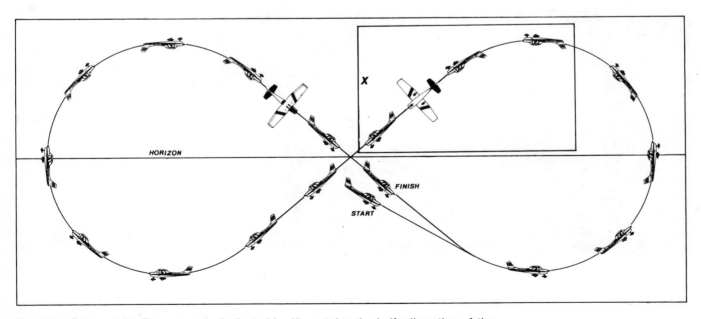

Fig. 5-5. Cuban eight. The rectangle (indicated by *X*) contains the half-roll portion of the maneuver. (See also Figs. 5-6 and 5-7.)

back pressure. The model may be used to demonstrate the Cuban eight completely at least once, but the explanation may concentrate on just half the maneuver.

Your instructor may handle the throttle at first, and as before you can expect a temporary slight decline in performance when *you* start using the throttle. It probably won't be so noticeable as earlier in your training, since you've had more practice at using power in the loop and cloverleaf.

As noted, an *aileron roll* is used to roll upright on the down side of the Cuban eight, starting at the 30°-nose-down (inverted) point; the nose transcribes a helix as you roll, completing the half roll with the nose down at a 45° angle (Figs. 5-6 and 5-7). This means that you will be firmer in the seat than would be the case if the roll was delayed to the 45°-nose-down point and held on that point on the ground as you rolled. With the latter technique you would use cross-control (rudder opposite to the roll) at the beginning and noticeable

forward pressure and moving toward negative g's at the first part of the roll. This latter method looks better from the ground but you'll feel more comfortable at first using the *half aileron roll* in the Cuban eight; you should also later be able to do the slow-roll technique discussed in a following section on the coordination exercise.

You can expect a requirement for an unusual (to you) amount of "forward" pressure at the beginning and throughout the roll. There are three main reasons for relaxing back pressure (or adding forward pressure):

1. *As the nose reaches the position of 30° below the horizon, the back pressure should be relaxed even more than it was for the "common" loop—in order to stop the loop.* (The roll is begun at this point.) Late or too-little relaxation will allow the nose to be too low when the roll is completed and a Cuban eight suddenly

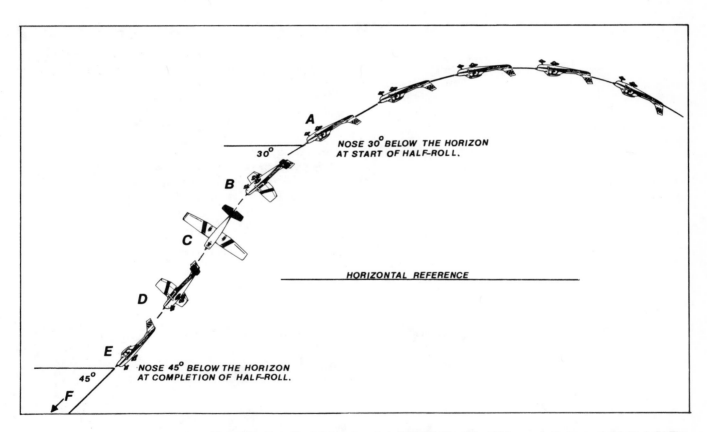

Fig. 5-6. Details of the rectangle in Fig. 5-5. (See Fig. 5-7 for cockpit views of points *A–F.*) The nose traces a helix from 30° down (inverted) to 45° down (upright). At the point where the back pressure would be started again in the loop *(A)*, start a half roll and release *more* back pressure as the airplane rolls. As the roll continues *(B)*, slightly increased forward pressure may be needed. Most aerobatic trainees tend to slack off on the forward pressure at *C*, and the nose is allowed to move to the right (in a left roll) of the reference line. This slacking off is one of the major causes of being off-heading at the end of the maneuver. In addition to the forward pressure being an important factor for directional precision, the increasing of top (left) rudder is needed to maintain heading as the roll is completed *(D)*. Forward pressure is needed at *E* to keep the nose from pitching up, which would result in a too-low airspeed for the next loop. As the airspeed reaches the proper value *(F)*, bring the nose up through the horizon for the second loop portion of the maneuver.

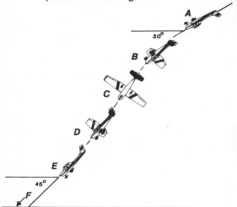

Fig. 5-7. Half roll of a Cuban eight as seen from the cockpit. Views **A–F** would be seen at points *A–F* in Fig. 5-6.

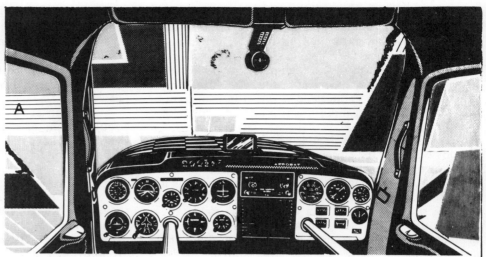

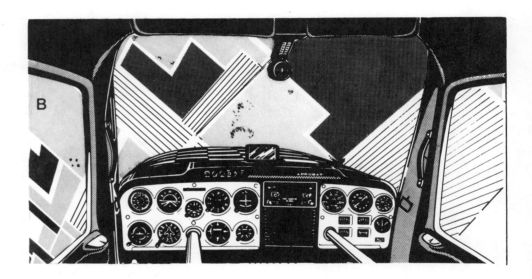

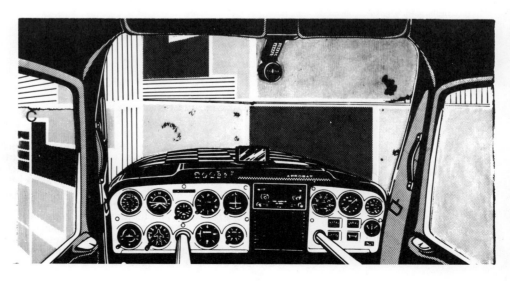

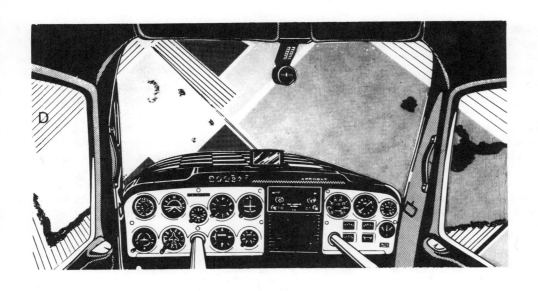

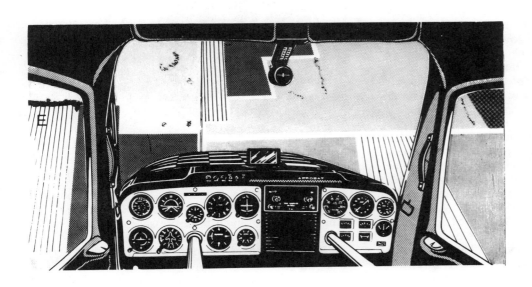

turns into a cloverleaf. This can be seen with the model.

2. *As the roll continues and the wing attitude approaches a vertical bank, the airplane will want to turn; relaxation of back pressure or adding forward pressure, as required for a particular airplane, stops this.* If after a half roll to the left the nose is pointed to the right of the road, you'll find that one of the causes was the lack of forward pressure (or decreased back pressure) at 90° of bank, allowing a turn. The other major factor in this case can be a lack of left rudder in the final 45° of roll. Since any problem caused by the lack of forward pressure occurs halfway in the roll, it is sometimes overlooked as a reason for heading problems at the completion. As noted earlier, a good aid in maintaining heading is the application of opposite rudder just as the half roll is started, followed by rudder *with* the aileron. This maneuver, which is more of a half slow roll than an aileron roll, is the best way to keep the nose lined up precisely, but the half aileron roll with its helix and more positive g's is still usually the best introduction. A problem at the end of any maneuver is often the result of a slipup at the beginning or middle, particularly in aerobatics. In other words, if you are *ending* the maneuver off-heading or having other trouble, don't ignore earlier factors that could have started the problem.

3. *When the roll is completed and the nose is pointed down at a 45° angle, it will tend to pitch up as the airspeed increases,* so the slight forward pressure must be continued after the roll is completed and the airplane approaches the desired pull-up airspeed.

You can expect that at one time or another your initial forward pressure will be too great and the engine may temporarily quit, but the roll should be continued. The engine will pick up power again, you can be sure.

PROCEDURE IN THE CUBAN EIGHT. Pick a straight stretch of road or section line and line up over it. Look around to make sure that somebody else hasn't decided to practice Cuban eights (or other maneuvers) on this same stretch.

Lower the nose (wings level) to a 45° angle to attain the recommended speed (120 K for the Aerobat). Ease the throttle back to prevent engine overspeed. Initiate a smooth pull-up and smoothly open the throttle so that full power is being developed as the nose is pointed straight up. A check will show 3.5 g's resulting from a proper pull-up. (Again, don't read the g meter while doing the action.)

Continue the loop, pulling positive g's and relaxing back pressure at the 30°-nose-up (inverted) position as usual for a loop. When the nose is pointed *down* at a 30° angle (the airplane inverted), release more back pressure and do a half aileron roll to the upright attitude (45°-nose-down). A half roll to the left is easier at first.

Keep the nose down at the 45° angle until the airspeed is again at the entry lead speed (check that rpm). Repeat the loop and half roll.

With most airplanes, including the Aerobat, you'll normally have time to complete the roll before needing to retard the throttle, but not if you're woolgathering or conducting a postmortem of the first half of the maneuver as you dive.

After you've completed the Cuban eight, review it as you climb back to the starting altitude. As an aerobatic devotee, you can generally think of the rest period between maneuvers also as *a time to climb.*

The use of a long, straight stretch of road, railroad, or section line cannot be overemphasized. You can see you're getting off-heading as it occurs and can start making corrections early.

Fig. 5-8 shows the numbers on the g meter after a Cuban eight. With practice you can do a Cuban eight without getting down to 0 g, holding it to 0.5 at the lowest value.

Fig. 5-8. Indications on the accelerometer (g meter) after a successful Cuban eight in the Aerobat, using half aileron rolls.

Common Errors in the Cuban Eight

1. Committing any of the errors associated with the loop, such as not enough back pressure at the beginning and/or too much back pressure at the top of the loop so that buffeting occurs.

2. Staring over the nose instead of checking the wing tips(s).

3. Applying back pressure or not enough forward pressure throughout the half-roll portion of the maneuver, causing deviation from the reference heading.

4. Tending to overdo the push-and-roll aspect after making common error 3 and being told about it a couple of times by the instructor—turning it in your mind to PUSH and roll, with plenty of PUSH but somewhat neglecting the roll. This can result in you and the instructor hanging on your harnesses, the engine hesitating, and little or no progress being made in roll. The instructor will most likely indicate that you are remiss in that regard. The best way to take care of the problem is to think of the forward pressure coming in with the roll initiation and smoothly continuing until the half roll is completed. You may tend to slack off the forward pressure as the roll progresses, allowing the airplane to end up off-heading and in a too-shallow dive.

5. Not completing the roll at a 45°-nose-down attitude—having the nose too high or low in the dive. Usually after you've done a session of cloverleafs it will tend to be too low.

6. Using too much initial aileron deflection, resulting in a buffet or an aileron stall (Aerobat).

7. Not using enough top rudder (rudder in direction of roll) as the roll is completed, allowing the airplane to get off-heading at that point.

8. Neglecting to retard the throttle as the airspeed picks up in the dive(s).

AND MORE PRACTICE OF THE CUBAN EIGHT. *To repeat*: Forward pressure is needed starting at the 30°-nose-down (inverted) position, and continued, for three reasons:

1. To stop the loop.
2. To stop any turn away from the reference (the airplane will want to turn the way it's banked).
3. To stop the pitch-up as the roll is completed and the airspeed is high.

Don't expect great things with the Cuban eight even after you have done, say, two dozen of them. Your later tendencies may be to cheat a little on the final 45°-nose-down attitude; you'll tend to have the dive too shallow, particularly if you are doing a series of maneuvers and/or have a minimum-altitude restriction.

If you pass through your own wake turbulence in the second dive on the Cuban eight, you generally have good control of the vertical plane of the maneuver. Of course, some individuals can do a *three*-dimensional Cuban eight—all over the sky—and somehow still manage to cross their own wake turbulence. This is similar to the example of the 720° power turn in which the altitude goes wild but wake turbulence is somehow encountered as the airplane recrosses an altitude. If you are flying through *somebody else's* wake turbulence while doing Cuban eights, you may be in for a little trouble. (Look around!)

You'll know that your progress in the Cuban eight—and aerobatics in general—is going great when you're heading earthward, *inverted,* at a 30–45° angle, and the only thing you're worried about is keeping lined up with that road as you start and continue the roll.

After the flight the instructor will review general problems of the Cuban eight, possibly demonstrating the entire maneuver using the model. You may be surprised to find you've been doing the Cuban eight mechanically, and seemingly well, throughout the flight but aren't able to "see" it. Your instructor may have you use the model and explain the maneuver, so that before you leave the airport you'll have the idea firmed up. Otherwise, the wrong concepts may be allowed to jell for a few days.

THE IMMELMANN

The Immelmann is a maneuver named for World War I German fighter pilot Max Immelmann. It consists of a half loop with a half roll at the top, so that the flight path is changed 180° with (if all goes well) a gain in altitude (Fig. 5-9). It is an excellent maneuver for developing good planning and coordination.

Fig. 5-9. Immelmann. See Fig. 5-10(A–E) for the views from the cockpit. The insert shows the "classic" maneuver. (From *The Flight Instructor's Manual*)

START THE HALF ROLL

EASE THE NOSE OVER TO PICK UP THE ENTRY SPEED

When you start doing Immelmanns you may invent maneuvers not generally seen. For instance, there is the "sky-suspended Immelmann," a maneuver in which you stop the nose (inverted) at a too-high attitude as speed rapidly disappears and the ailerons are centered (in awe). The earth and sky appear suspended (inverted in position, of course). The engine loses power (if you aren't flying an airplane with an inverted system), and it becomes your duty to put things back to rights. The feeling is that the airplane is fluttering down like a clean-shot duck. It takes a little altitude, plus maybe a little time, for airplane and occupant(s) to get back to normal.

Another variation is a "combination Cuban eight and Immelmann." The nose position at the end of the maneuver is too low for an Immelmann and too high for a Cuban eight. Quite a few of these are done in aerobatic courses.

A LOOK AT THE IMMELMANN. The Immelmann is a combination of a half loop and half roll. While more powerful airplanes may gain altitude during its execution (and some people do literally *execute* it, as in a firing squad), in most trainer aircraft you will be satisfied if the initial altitude is again reached. But it is more important to develop the proper techniques than to worry too much about altitude gain. Like the Cuban eight, a plane through the flight path of the airplane should be perpendicular to the earth's surface.

This maneuver is one of the best for flying the airplane through a wide range of airspeeds and doing a precise half roll at speeds approaching the stall. The Immelmann is one of the more difficult maneuvers for the low-powered airplane because of the low speed at the point of roll.

PROCEDURE IN THE IMMELMANN. Line up over a long road or section line so that a reference for both directions of flight can be used. If such a long, straight reference is not available, pick a prominent object on the horizon and turn the airplane so that the tail is lined up with it. As the half-loop portion of the Immelmann is nearing completion, you'll use the reference to make the half (aileron) roll.

Check the area for other airplanes and lower the nose to establish the recommended Aerobat airspeed of 130 K (150 mph), or what *your* airplane uses for the Immelmann. Retard the throttle as necessary to stay below the red line on the tach. Initiate a smooth pull-up and gradually open the throttle so that full power is developed by the time the vertical position is reached. Watch the wing tip(s) as for any loop-type maneuver. Check for the horizon as the inverted position is approached. Note that 4.0 g's result from a proper pull-up in the Aerobat.

There are two ways to make a half roll in the Immelmann:

1. Start a left aileron roll when the nose is approximately 30° above the horizon (inverted). Allow the nose to move smoothly down to the horizon as the half roll is done. Use slight forward pressure during the first part of the roll and at the 90° roll point be prepared to *increase* the forward pressure to keep the nose from being off to the right as the roll ends (as is necessary for the half roll in the Cuban eight). During the last 45° of roll, be prepared to apply more left rudder; as the roll is being completed, back pressure is used to keep the nose in the attitude required to maintain level flight. Fig. 5-10A–E shows the aileron roll as seen from the cockpit in the sequence of Fig. 5-9A–E.

2. As the airplane approaches the inverted position (about 15° above the horizon), use forward pressure to stop the loop and use left aileron and right rudder as necessary to keep the nose on the point. As the bank becomes vertical, apply rudder *with* the ailerons. Increase the rudder deflection and/or apply back pressure as the roll is completed. This procedure may give you a

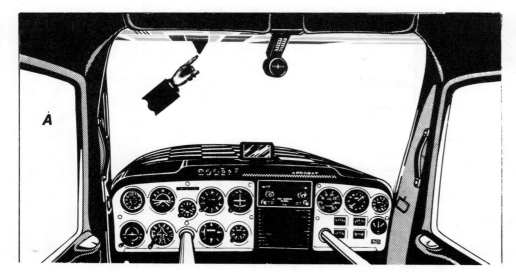

Fig. 5-10. A–E. Immelmann, as seen from the cockpit during the 180° aileron roll. Compare the airplane positions (A–E) in Fig. 5-9 with A–E here.

(A) As the airplane reaches the 30°-nose-"up" position (inverted) and the "prominent object" comes into sight, an aileron roll is started (push and roll). You may not be so lucky as to have a giant hand pointing out the reference. It's possible, also, that *your* practice area does not have a large, black triangle on the horizon for a reference as shown in this series. As you gain more experience, you can look "up" through the skylight at the 45° pitch (inverted) position and so pick up the reference early.

(B) The roll continues.

(C) You may have to concentrate on forward pressure here.

(D) Start applying more top (left) rudder and *back* pressure at this point.

(E) The airplane is just above a stall as the wings are leveled.

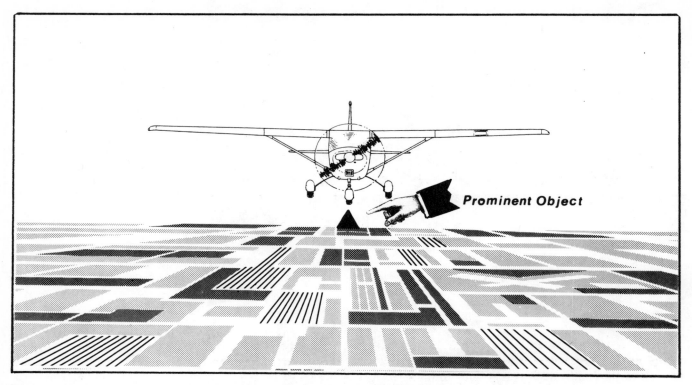

Fig. 5-11. Putting the tail of the airplane on a prominent object to do an Immelmann. Looking back to line up the tail with the reference when you're strapped in and with a parachute on can lead to a stiff neck, but look around anyway.

little more "lightness" on top and some engine hesitation as compared to (1). More about this in the sections on applying the coordination exercise to the Cuban eight and Immelmann. A comparison of techniques (1) and (2) is shown in Fig. 5-17. A roll to the left is easier for the Aerobat and most lower-powered U.S. airplanes, but after a while you might want to try some right rolls.

One thing you'll discover as you do more aerobatics is that a good horizon is required for the loop-type maneuvers. Things are happening pretty fast at first, and if it's a hazy day with only a faint horizon, you'll most likely miss it. This isn't quite so critical in the loop, Cuban eight, or cloverleaf because you will also be using ground references to complete the maneuver. With the Immelmann, however, the horizon is very important since you will be using it to stop the loop and start the roll.

Fig. 5-11 demonstrates picking a prominent object and turning until it's on the tail. Be sure that it *is* an object on or near the horizon, or a cloud that is easily distinguishable when you are looking for it from an inverted position. Picking one of a dozen similar cumulus clouds can lead to confusion; you won't know whether you rolled out on the prechosen cloud or one 30° (or more) from it.

The instructor probably won't push you too hard at first to roll out on an exact heading. You'll be allowed to get used to stopping the loop and rolling out at the lower speed.

Fig. 5-12 shows the accelerometer reading after completing an Immelmann in the Aerobat, using the first type of the half-roll technique discussed earlier.

Common Errors in the Immelmann

1. Committing any of the common errors associated with the loop, cloverleaf, and Cuban eight (throttle handling, back pressure, etc.).

2. Applying too-abrupt forward pressure at the top of the loop—creating a "sky-suspended" situation. (This is the point at which you find out where the mechanic left the pliers.)

3. Initiating the half roll too early or too late—the timing may be off even if the roll is smooth, which is particularly a problem if the horizon is not well defined. If a reference point is "put on the tail," as mentioned earlier, you may "lose" it when time comes for the rollout.

Fig. 5-12. Post-Immelmann accelerometer reading.

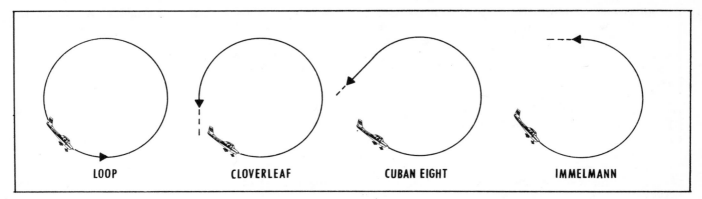

Fig. 5-13. Loop-roll combinations in the order of difficulty (*left to right*).

4. Having line-up problems after the roll-out. After you've practiced a number of Immelmanns using coordinated aileron and rudder all the way, the instructor will show you that the application of opposite rudder at the beginning of the roll (with coordinated rudder and aileron later) can be a good aid in final heading control.

MORE ABOUT THE IMMELMANN. As noted, the roll at the top of the Immelmann is best done to the left with the Aerobat as with most U.S.-built airplanes. Your instructor will have you rolling left, at least for the first few times. For right rolls you might add 10 K and use 140 KIAS (160 mph) for better control at the top.

Getting back to the earlier 130-K (150-mph) Immelmann, in the Aerobat you can expect to complete the roll-out at about 200 ft below the altitude at which the dive was started. Again, though, the idea is to develop your technique so that when you fly an airplane with more power, altitude will be gained in the maneuver. You'll get the feeling in the pull-up and roll out at the top that plenty of altitude *was* gained (which it was—from the bottom of the loop).

With practice and working out your smoothness, an Immelmann can be done in the Aerobat with limits of +3.5 g's on the pull-up and +0.5 g's at the roll-out (or very close to the initial loop numbers with an aileron-roll-type completion).

Fig. 5-13 shows the loop-roll combinations in general order of difficulty. You will notice that the loop is being "opened up" more in each case.

THE COORDINATION EXERCISE

In the discussion of the Cuban eight and Immelmann it was suggested that to roll upright from the inverted position a cross-control method could be used, such as left aileron and right rudder, and then changing to left rudder (with the aileron) as the roll is completed. This procedure is more of a slow roll (rolling *on* a point—not covered as a maneuver in this book) than an aileron roll (rolling *around* a point). After you feel comfortable with the loop-roll-combination maneuvers, your instructor may introduce this procedure.

The coordination exercise is a good way to get the feel of cross-controlling and keeping the nose on a point. The maneuver consists of pointing the nose at a reference on the horizon and rolling from bank to bank, keeping the nose pinned on the reference. The coordination exercise is sometimes incorrectly referred to as a "Dutch roll." (Dutch roll, a stability and control term, is a condition in which the nose yaws as the airplane rolls from bank to bank; you want to keep the nose on the point, here.)

It's a good maneuver for introducing the idea of "flying on your side" in a slip. In keeping the nose on

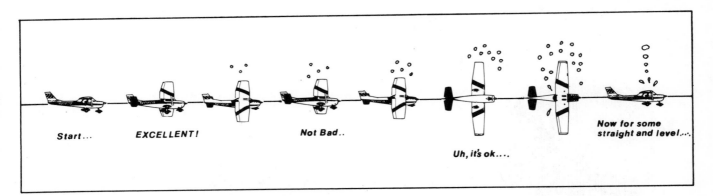

Fig. 5-14. The instructor may suggest limiting the coordination exercise.

the point some sideslip must occur (if even for a very short while) when rolling from one bank to the other.

It's best to start with shallow banks and then progress to medium and then steeper ones. There will be some nose movement, but you should keep it to a minimum.

Here you'll see fully that coordination, as far as aerobatics are concerned, is making the airplane do what you want it to do, sometimes with the ball in the turn and slip or turn coordinator trying to get out of the instrument.

A note of caution: For some people a coordination exercise, if extended, can cause nausea problems, so it's best not to spend too much time on it in one sitting or NSMFA (see Chap. 1) may occur (Fig. 5-14).

PRACTICING THE COORDINATION EXERCISE. Set up normal, level cruise at 2300 rpm (2500 rpm) and pick a prominent reference on the horizon (or a particular cloud, if it's hazy and the horizon is hard to find).

Start the maneuver by applying left aileron and left rudder, as in starting a turn. Before the nose has a chance to move, apply right rudder so that the point is held. Then apply right aileron and more right rudder and roll into a right bank, stopping the turn tendency with opposite (left) rudder.

Continue the exercise until you are able to keep the nose on the point without undue yawing movements, or until you or the instructor decide that it's time to move onward and upward to bigger and better things. You'll need to coordinate the elevator with the other controls, particularly at steeper banks.

You may want to break up the practice into parts of several flights. As indicated earlier, start with shallow banks, then work into medium and steep ones. Repeat the maneuver at slower speeds such as approach or slow flight speeds to see the requirement for a different coordination procedure (more rudder deflection) at the lower speeds.

While this isn't a precision maneuver as far as

maintaining altitude is concerned, any significant changes in altitude mean the exercise is being done improperly. It's good training to keep a check on the altitude as part of your performance requirements.

In addition to giving you another look at roll procedures in the Cuban eight and Immelmann, the ability to do good coordination exercises will be a great help when you start working on four- and eight-point rolls (see Chap. 6).

Common Errors in the Coordination Exercise

1. Failure to apply opposite rudder in time, or insufficient use of opposite rudder—the nose moves from the point.

2. Forgetting that the elevator is part of the action of coordination.

3. Excessive gain or loss of altitude during the series.

APPLYING THE EXERCISE TO THE CUBAN EIGHT. The half-roll technique described in the Cuban eight earlier in the chapter was that of the aileron roll, starting with the nose 30° below the horizon (inverted) and ending with the nose 45° below the horizon (upright). The flight path was a helix or corkscrew (well, *half* a corkscrew) turn, and there was no cross-controlling involved.

The idea now is to stop the nose-down movement at the 45° down point and then roll around that line (Fig. 5-15). You may expect to be in a range of from +0.5 to −1.0 g at point A in Fig. 5-15; it will depend on your enthusiasm and skill level.

The procedure: The loop portion is the same except that any roll is delayed until reaching the 45°-nose-down point (inverted), at which the loop is stopped by forward pressure as required and the half roll is started. Look at the points A through E in Fig. 5-15.

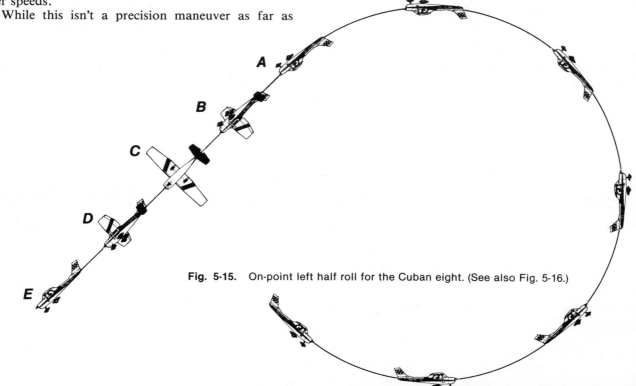

Fig. 5-15. On-point left half roll for the Cuban eight. (See also Fig. 5-16.)

At point *A,* move the control wheel forward until the nose is stopped on the 45° downline (inverted). A few degrees of lead may be necessary; for instance, starting the forward pressure at the 30°- or 35°-nosedown point (depending again on your experience and rapidity of "push").

At point *B,* use left aileron (for a *left* roll) to start the roll and with some airplanes apply *right* rudder as necessary to keep the nose on the "point" on the ground along the 45° line. Using aileron alone (no left *or* right rudder) as the roll starts works well with the Aerobat,

which has about the right amount of adverse yaw with aileron alone to keep the nose on the point. You'll bring in left rudder as the roll continues. As the roll goes on further, ease off the right rudder (if used) while applying forward pressure. To pin it on the point, bring in left rudder as the roll continues.

At point *C,* approximately the 90°-bank point, strong *left* rudder is needed for some airplanes to keep the nose from dropping (you can feel the slip). Keep applying forward pressure.

At point *D,* continue to use left rudder with the left

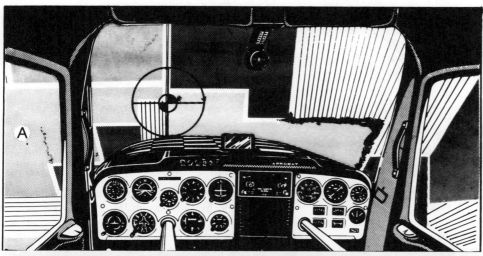
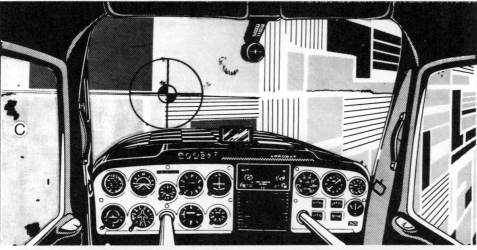
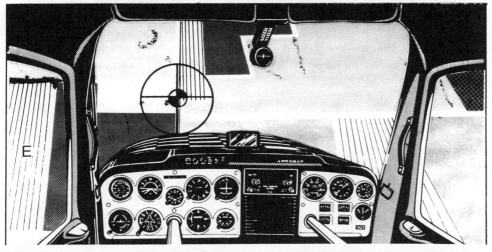

Fig. 5-16. On-point half roll as seen from the cockpit. Views **A, C,** and **E** are seen at those same points in Fig. 5-15. Note that the roll is to the right in this case.

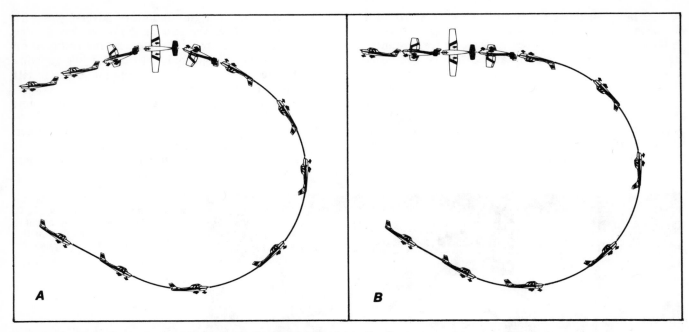

Fig. 5-17. Immelmann roll-outs. **(A)** Aileron half roll. **(B)** On-point half roll.

aileron to complete the roll (still applying forward pressure).

At point *E,* use forward pressure as necessary to keep the nose on the point as the airspeed increases to 120 K (or your recommended airspeed) for the next half of the Cuban eight.

Trying the cross-controlling at the beginning of the maneuver may be a little like patting your head and rubbing your stomach, but you'll soon get the feel of it. Also, although the movement toward negative g's could feel uncomfortable at first and engines without inverted fuel systems could lose power, these won't be worry factors after a couple of practice sessions.

Fig. 5-16 shows the procedure as seen from the cockpit with a *right* half roll.

**Common Errors in Applying the Exercise
to the Cuban Eight**

1. Using too much opposite rudder as the roll starts—pulling the nose well off-heading.

2. Not applying enough forward pressure throughout the roll.

3. Using poor coordination when transitioning to the proroll rudder as the roll proceeds.

APPLYING THE EXERCISE TO THE IMMELMANN. The same basic procedure of roll can be used for the Immelmann. At the top of the loop portion you'll let the nose get lower before starting the roll. Don't start the roll at the 30°-nose-up point (inverted) discussed in the earlier description of the Immelmann.

As the 15°-nose-up-point (inverted) is reached,

move in with smooth forward pressure to stop the loop.

Use left aileron (for example), and no rudder (or slight right rudder) in the Aerobat, to do a half roll at a point on the horizon.

As the roll progresses toward the vertical bank position make a smooth transition to left rudder as the second 90° of roll is completed.

Relax the forward pressure used during the inverted part of the roll and then apply back pressure to keep the nose on the reference point as the airplane completes its roll to the upright position.

Expect some "hanging around" and power loss for the no-inverted system engine. This is (again) where you will find that no matter how tight you thought the belt and shoulder harness were, they're now not tight enough.

Fig. 5-17 compares the two types of rolls at the top of the Immelmann.

**Common Errors in Applying the Exercise
to the Immelmann**

1. Not using enough forward pressure at the 15° point (inverted).

2. Having problems with the cross-control (usually too much opposite rudder the first few times).

3. Relaxing the back pressure while the airplane is still inverted during the roll process.

4. Having trouble with the transition to pro-roll rudder.

5. Not coming in with the required back pressure as the airplane rolls upright.

Fig. 5-18.   Spin, loop, aileron roll, and snap combination.

SPINS AND COMBINATIONS

Fig. 5-18 shows a good combination of maneuvers to use after the spin has been introduced. You can do a one-and-one-half-turn spin using a road as reference, followed by a loop, aileron roll, and snap roll. You can, for instance, start off by doing a spin followed by only *one* of the three other maneuvers and then gradually work up to the full system.

You can combine the spin with any of the maneuvers you'll have in the course. The spin doesn't have to be first in the combination, but it is a good one to use in picking up extra airspeed after the recovery because of the nose-down attitude. You would not likely follow a loop or aileron roll with a spin because the interval required for the airspeed to decay down to a safe spin-entry value would be too long, and the sequential concept would be lost. A spin *following* an Immelmann (and it sometimes does, whether wanted or not) or a snap roll (and sometimes this accidentally happens, too) makes better sense.

6
MORE VARIATIONS AND COMBINATIONS

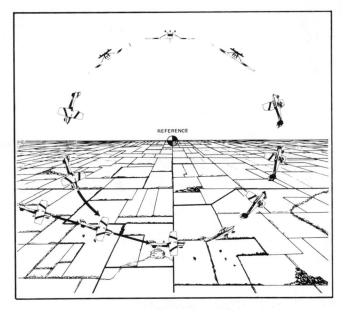

Fig. 6-1. Barrel roll as seen from the side of the initial dive. (From *The Flight Instructor's Manual*)

BARREL ROLL

The barrel roll is a precise maneuver in which the airplane is rolled around an imaginary point at 45° to the original flight path. A positive-g level is maintained throughout the maneuver, and the ball in the turn and slip or turn coordinator stays in the middle (it says here).

You may wonder why the barrel roll is mentioned this late, since it appears to be so simple. Well, for one thing, it's a precise maneuver requiring particular airplane attitudes at particular reference points, and it can be difficult to do properly at first.

This maneuver can be considered an exaggeration of the wingover, only instead of starting to shallow the bank at the 90° position the pilot must steepen it continually until the airplane has *rolled* 360° and is back on the original heading at the completion of the maneuver. The rate of roll must be much greater than used for the wingover because the airplane must be in a vertical bank at 45° of "turn" and must be inverted at the 90° change of heading. The roll and turn are continued until the airplane is headed in the original direction with the wings level. Fig. 6-1 shows the barrel roll.

From *behind* this maneuver looks as though the airplane is being flown around the outside of a barrel. This is a very good maneuver for gaining confidence and keeping oriented while flying in balanced flight. Good coordination is required to do the barrel roll properly, and pilots show an improvement in that area after a session of these. The barrel roll is generally more difficult and requires more precision than the aileron roll, and you may have to put some extra work in on this one.

The barrel roll is definitely one of the better maneuvers for improving your orientation because, unlike the other aerobatic maneuvers covered thus far, the barrel roll requires a *constantly* changing bank *and* pitch (with attendant changing airspeeds) and a radical change from the initial heading (90°) while the airplane

is rolling. The average pilot probably will be looking at the wing tip at a time when the nose should be checked, or vice versa. When you are able to stay well oriented in the barrel roll, you are ready to move on to the reverse Cuban eight or reverse cloverleaf.

PROCEDURE IN THE BARREL ROLL. Fig. 6-2A–E shows some points in the barrel roll as seen from the cockpit and from behind the airplane.

Make sure the area is clear and pick a reference on the horizon off the wing tip, as for the wingover and lazy eight.

Set the throttle to low-cruise rpm and ease the nose over to pick up about 10 K more than used for the wingover, or set up the airspeed used for a loop, whichever is higher. For the Aerobat an entry speed of 120 K (140 mph) is suggested. Reduce power in the dive as necessary to avoid exceeding the rpm red line. Adding full power as the bank approaches 90° will aid the maneuver.

Smoothly pull the nose up and start a coordinated climbing turn (it will have to be at a much faster rate than was used for the wingover) toward the reference point (Fig. 6-2A). (Assume a roll to the left.)

Fig. 6-2. Barrel roll as seen from the cockpit and from behind the airplane. **(A)** The nose reaches the level position. **(B)** Turned 45° to the left from the original heading. **(C)** At 90° of turn, 180° of roll (the reference is seen briefly over the nose). **(D)** The nose is pointing 45° to the left of the original flight line. **(E)** In level flight, resuming cruise, on the original heading (the reference again off the wing tip).

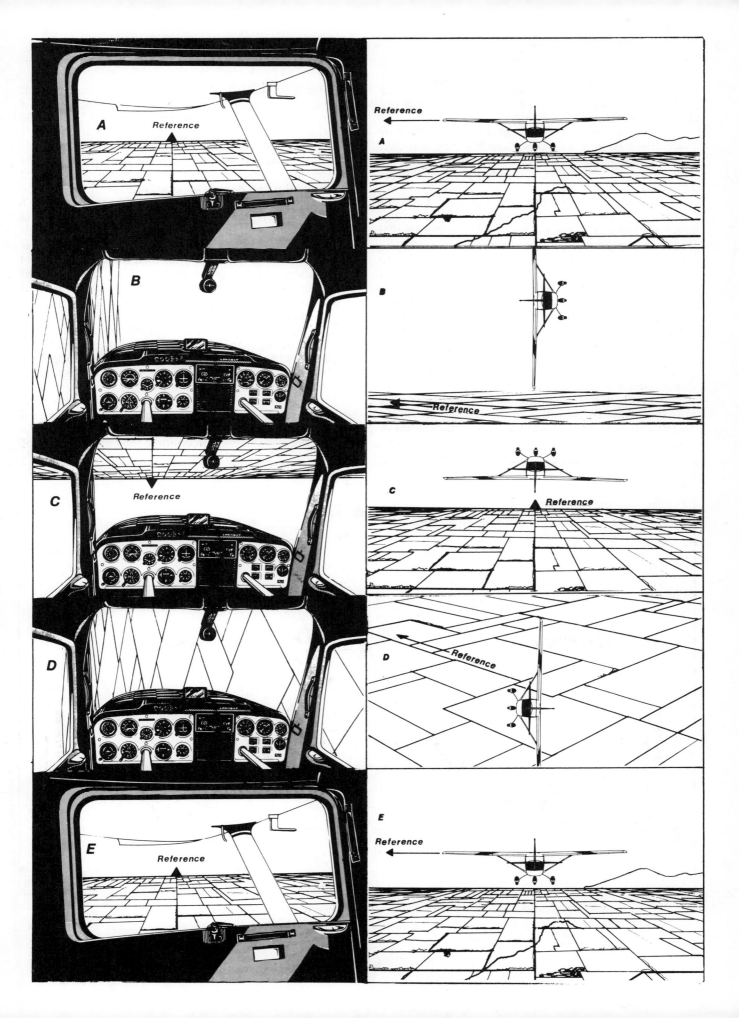

When the nose is 45° from the original heading (Fig 6-2B), it should be at its highest pitch attitude and the left bank should be vertical.

When the nose is at 90° from the original heading (180° of roll), you should be looking (momentarily) directly at the reference point that was originally off the wing tip—from a completely inverted position (Fig. 6-2C).

When the airplane heading is again 45° from the original (Fig. 6-2D), the bank is vertical but you will be in a *right* bank as far as the ground is concerned; that is, the right wing will be pointing straight down at this instant of roll. The nose will be at its *lowest* pitch attitude at this point.

Continue the roll to wings-level flight as the nose is raised back to the cruise attitude. Make necessary power adjustments and resume cruise on the original heading. The reference should be properly repositioned off the wing tip (Fig. 6-2E).

The maneuver must be symmetrical; the nose must go as far above the horizon as below. The barrel roll requires definite checkpoints to ensure that the airplane is at the correct attitude throughout. It is interesting to note that if the barrel roll is to the left, all of the airplane's path is to the left and above the original line of flight at the pull-up and the airplane's nose is always

pointed to the left of the original flight line (until it merges again at the completion of the maneuver). The opposite occurs, naturally, for the barrel roll to the right.

Another method of doing a barrel roll is to pick a reference on the horizon, turn the airplane 45° to the reference point, and proceed to make a wide roll around this *real* point. One disadvantage of this method for the newcomer is that it depends on the pilot's own judgment of how large the orbit around the point should be. As an introduction to the maneuver the first method is usually better, but you may come to prefer the second and work out your own technique. Another variation used in aerobatic competition is close to the aileron roll described earlier in the book (the nose varies 40° rather than 90° from its original heading).

You may rest assured that you will "lose" the reference point the first couple of barrel rolls. The wing of the Aerobat, and of other high-wing aerobatic airplanes, will obscure it as you start the roll and approach the 45°-of-turn position (90° bank); if you have set up the proper roll and pitch rate it will soon reappear. Most people start out by staring over the nose (remember those first loops?), seeing nothing but sky and not knowing what is going on.

Fig. 6-3 is a two-dimensional look at the barrel roll

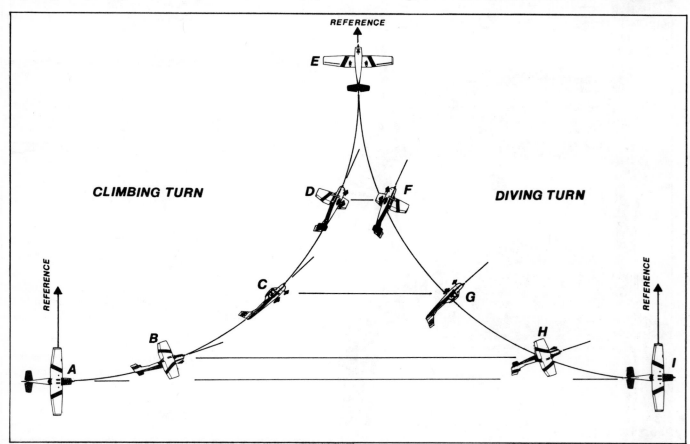

Fig. 6-3.   Left barrel roll: general path, bank attitudes, and headings in a two-dimensional view.

as it would be seen from directly above. The first half might be viewed as a climbing turn with a 90° direction change coupled with 180° of roll. The last half is a diving turn with another 180° of roll (in the same direction, back to upright) along with another 90° of turn, back to the original heading. Note that headings are "paired," although the airplane's bank attitudes may be different in most cases (point B = H, C = G, and D = F as far as headings from the original course are concerned; points A and I are the same heading, airspeed, and altitude). The reference should be far enough out on the horizon so that there should be no angular change between sights at points A, E, and I. You may want to get a model and go through the maneuver to compare headings and banks here. Point C has the highest pitch attitude, point G the lowest.

Common Errors in the Barrel Roll

1. Not pulling the nose high enough in the first 45° of roll in the maneuver, which means that the highest and lowest nose positions are not symmetrical in relation to the horizon.

2. Not maintaining a *constant* rate of roll (watch for this problem in particular). Usually things are fine at the 45° position, the nose at its highest pitch and the bank is vertical, but as you approach the position of 90° of direction change you find you are not going to be completely inverted at that point and have to rush things a bit to make it. The usual reason for this situation is that you didn't maintain a constant rate of roll. Remember that the nose is up and the airspeed is slower in this segment of the maneuver, so the controls must be deflected more to get the same rate.

3. Letting the nose drop too rapidly after passing the 90° point—losing too much altitude and gaining excess airspeed.

4. Failing to roll out on the original heading—having the wing tip well ahead (or well behind) the reference when the maneuver is completed.

THE SNAP AT THE TOP OF A LOOP

The recommended speed for this maneuver in the Aerobat is 130 K (150 mph); for other aerobatic airplanes you might think in terms of adding 10–15 K to the normal loop entry speed. You'll tack on about an additional ½ g at the initial pull-up; one of the major errors is to "hold back" the control wheel with continuing g forces, getting a buffet as the inverted position is approached.

PROCEDURE IN THE SNAP AT THE TOP OF A LOOP.

The snap portion should be symmetrical, that is, with the snap beginning (Fig. 6-4, point X) and ending (point Y) at the proper points on the loop circle. Fig. 6-5 shows the steps in the snap at the top of a loop, as seen from the cockpit.

Clear the area. After lining up with a road or railroad, start the loop at 130 K (150 mph). Don't forget to add full power as the pitch attitude reaches vertical or the snap will be sloppy indeed. When the nose is 45° above the horizon (inverted) execute a snap roll to the left (full left rudder, simultaneous with full wheel back, then left aileron after the roll starts) (Figs. 6-4, point A, and 6-5A).

In Fig. 6-4, point B (and Fig. 6-5B), the airplane has completed one-half of the snap roll. (Remember, you started from the inverted position.)

Look out the left (lean over if necessary), and when the road, railroad, or section line reference comes into sight, start the snap roll recovery (full right rudder, wheel forward, and right aileron) (Figs. 6-4, point C, and 6-5C).

During the snap roll you will probably not know the airplane's attitude and position at any particular time. (One aerobatic trainee put it, "There was earth and sky and earth and sky and...."). The point is that when you are able to see the road, railroad, or section line appear in the left window again (assuming that the snap is to the left), initiate the recovery procedure, as the airplane will be at about the 270° of roll at that point.

As soon as the recovery is started, get back to looking over the nose to stop the snap and check for the completion of the loop. Complete the recovery. The airplane should *not* be pointed straight down (Figs. 6-4, point D, and 6-5D). Continue the loop, reducing the throttle and checking the line-up as the pullout is completed.

The snap at the top may not be as "brisk" as the normal snap roll because the rate of speed decay in the loop may catch you by surprise.

For higher-powered airplanes with a faster roll rate you may find that starting the snap with the nose lower (30°) gives a more symmetrical pattern.

You should use a model to "fly" the maneuver to make it clearer to see. For some reason some people have trouble with a snap roll that starts from an inverted position, not just because it seems to take longer to complete but because it seems unnatural and illegal to initiate it there.

Common Errors in the Snap at the Top of a Loop.

1. Not attaining enough airspeed for entry. This is a usual situation at first, since you'll tend to be somewhat reluctant to get the higher speed required and may have had this problem in the normal loop a couple of times. You might have to work on this for several of the maneuvers.

2. Having a poor loop pattern. The added airspeed can throw off the back-pressure technique so the loop is not "efficient" or the airspeed at the top will be too slow for a good snap. (Check the common errors in the loop again.)

3. Overspeeding the engine. You may be tense in this new maneuver and this, plus the fact that you are 10 K (or more) faster at this pitch attitude than the one in which you open the throttle for the loop, can cause

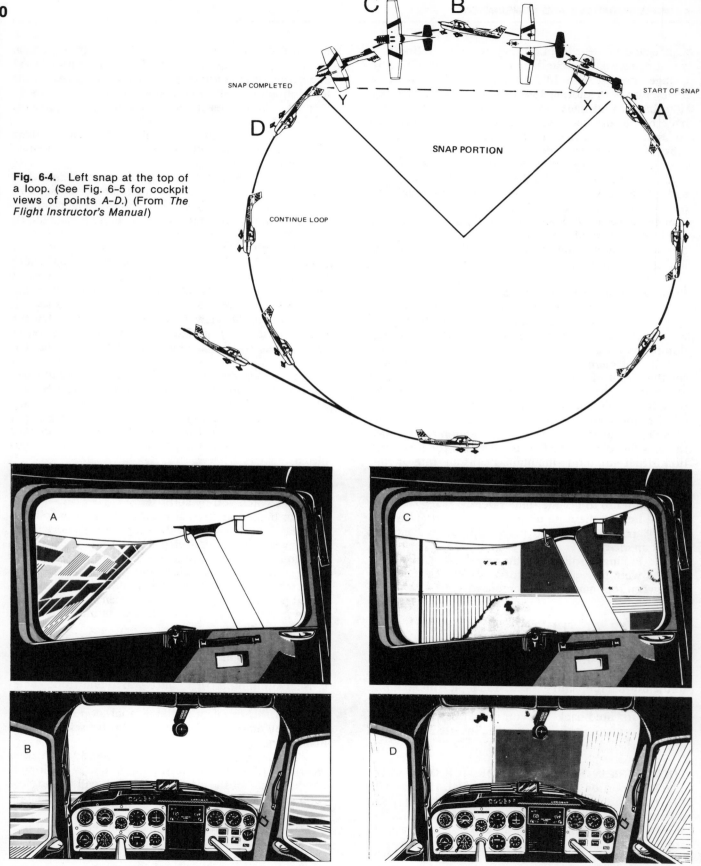

Fig. 6-4. Left snap at the top of a loop. (See Fig. 6-5 for cockpit views of points *A–D.*) (From *The Flight Instructor's Manual*)

Fig. 6-5. Snap at the top of a loop as seen from the cockpit. Views **A–D** are seen at those same points in Fig. 6-4.

such overspeeding. Keep the rpm below the red line.

4. Starting the snap too late—the nose is too low (inverted) at the point of snap initiation and the recovery is in a too-nose-low position. The airspeed will have decayed further because the airplane is nearer the top of the loop, and a sloppy nose-low recovery is encouraged by this, too.

5. Losing orientation during the snap. Most people have this problem to some extent, and for some it causes a great deal of trouble. A split-second delay in starting the recovery from a snap maneuver can mean that precision is lost.

6. *Not* relaxing back pressure enough as the snap roll is completed, which will contribute to a nose-low position when the loop portion is resumed.

7. Having a poor transition from the snap back to the loop—not flying the airplane in the last part of the loop. Some people are so pleased with a good snap that they'll spend some time mentally congratulating themselves while the rest of the maneuver falls apart.

8. Failing to reduce power on the back side of the loop. Things are occurring in rapid order, and this step may be forgotten during the commotion.

9. Starting recovery too soon—feeling that a snap roll started from an inverted position takes "longer" than the usual one.

THE REVERSE CUBAN EIGHT

The reverse Cuban eight differs from the normal Cuban eight in that the half roll is executed as the airplane is *climbing* at a 45° angle (Fig. 6-6).

PROCEDURE IN THE REVERSE CUBAN EIGHT. Choose a straight stretch of road, and after clearing the area, ease the nose over to pick up the recommended airspeed.

Bring the nose up smartly to a pitch of 45° above the horizon; add full power as the airspeed decreases (the power at this point helps keep a higher altitude at the bottom of the loop portion).

As the airspeed decreases, complete a half roll in either direction. Usually a hesitation and relaxation of back pressure (and maybe a slight forward pressure) before "pulling through" makes for a better-rounded loop portion, keeps the airspeed from being too high at the bottom, and stops excessive altitude loss. This hesitation can allow time for any correction of wing attitude before the loop starts. At this point (inverted), the skylights should be used to check (and correct as necessary) the line-up with the road. Fly the loop, using the normal procedures (throttle handling, control pressures, etc.), and bring the nose back up to the 45°-nose-up position to repeat the process.

The entry (pull-up) speed of this maneuver should be *at least* 10 K lower than that recommended for the "normal" Cuban eight so that the airspeed will be very low after the half roll is completed and the "fly through" (or loop portion) is started. For the Aerobat, start the pull-up at 100 K (110 mph). One of the commonest problems is not letting the airspeed decay low enough before flying the airplane through the loop portion.

Another problem that can arise in this maneuver is not bringing the nose up to the 45° position before the roll is started. The wing tip(s) is a useful aid for checking pitch attitude.

If you use the aileron-type half roll, expect a problem in heading to result. You may find that the airplane is not lining up with the reference road as the nose is "pulled down" through the loop portion and the type of roll can be a contributing factor. In the aileron roll the nose projects an orbit, starting at a reference point, and while at the completion of the 360° of roll the nose is

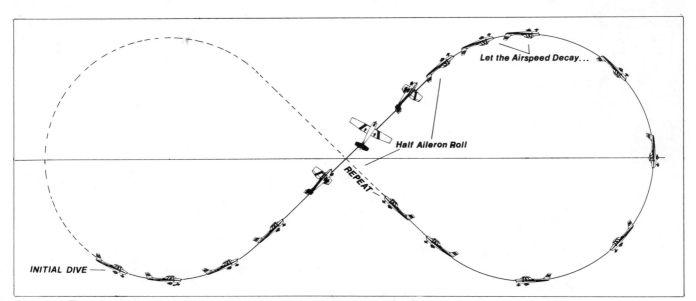

Fig. 6-6. Reverse Cuban eight. During the period of inverted flight (as the airspeed decays) move your head back to use the skylights to check, and correct, any problems with road line-up.

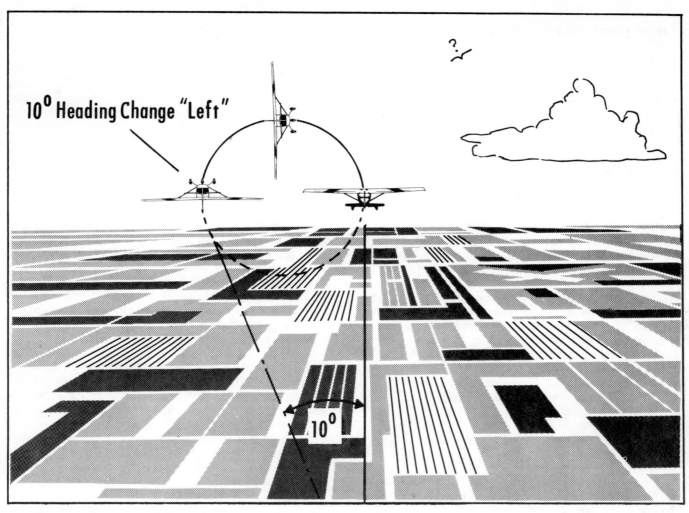

Fig. 6-7. Possible errors in line-up in the loop portion caused by doing a *half aileron* roll in the reverse Cuban eight. The dashed portion of the circle shows that the airplane would have returned to the original heading had the roll been continued.

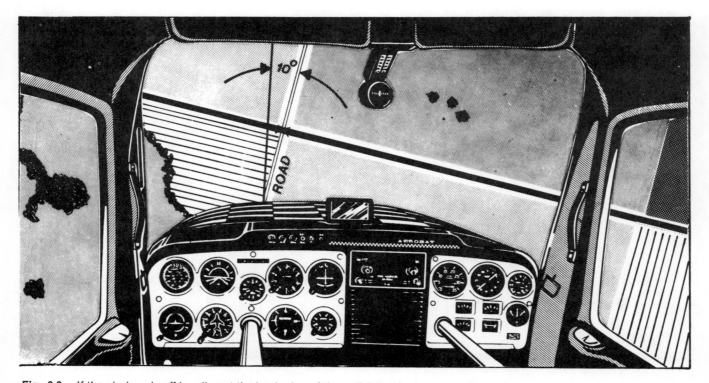

Fig. 6-8. If the airplane is off-heading at the beginning of the pull-through, the same original error will be shown by the reference (road). The error will be in the direction of roll.

again pointed *exactly* at the beginning reference (well, most of the time—okay, a few of the times), at 180° of roll the nose will be off laterally to the "left" of the original line, if a left roll is being made (and vice versa). Fig. 6-7 shows the idea.

You may suspect this is the problem if, as the loop portion is continued and the road comes back in view, the nose is pointed to the *left* of the road after a *left* roll was used (Fig. 6-8). There are two methods of correcting for the off-heading problem.

1. Use the half (180°) aileron roll and as the roll enters the last 30°, use rudder pressure in the direction of roll. If the half roll is to the left, then left rudder pressure is eased in as the last 30° of roll is being done. This will yaw the nose to line it up with the road or railroad reference as the half roll is completed.

2. The roll may be a cross-control type of effort (see the discussion of the Cuban eight and Immelmann in Chap. 5), starting with, say, left aileron alone (in the Aerobat) or using right rudder to keep the nose from moving and ending up inverted with rudder and ailerons neutral. You are rolling *on* an imaginary point 45° up, and if you do it properly, you won't have the problem of being off-heading that is possible with the aileron-roll-type entry.

Another cause of directional error is not having the wings level as the roll is stopped. Since the loop path is (or should be) perpendicular to the lateral axis, an off-heading problem like that shown in Fig. 6-9 results.

A third off-heading problem can be caused by improper correction for "torque" in the initial pull-up. The airplane will be slowing rapidly with full power used, so the heading may have a left heading error even before the roll is started because the high-pitch attitude of the nose obscures the horizon. Clouds may be used as references at this point (if available), and the heading can be flown using them in relation to the ground refer-

Fig. 6-9. Result of the wings not being level at the top of the loop of the reverse Cuban eight.

ence. Since in most areas there are very few days when the horizon is well defined, you'll be using references that are not on the horizon but will project to an imaginary point on the unseen horizon (Fig. 6-9). This can apply to all maneuvers.

Common Errors in the Reverse Cuban Eight

1. Not raising the nose high enough (45° above the horizon), resulting in a poorly executed maneuver and an excessive loss of altitude.

2. Allowing a too-high airspeed when the loop portion is started—a high airspeed at the bottom of the loop results. You may not have raised the nose high enough (common error 1) or pulled through too quickly, not allowing the airspeed to decay properly.

3. Line-up problems after the half roll is completed. Checking through the skylights while inverted will help avoid this problem.

4. Failing to retard the throttle as the airspeed picks up in the dive.

VARIATIONS OF THE REVERSE CUBAN EIGHT. The reverse Cuban eight may also be done using a half snap

roll at the 45° pitch position. The half-snap-roll entry means that you'll have to stop the snap almost as soon as it starts. A slight overshoot of roll (probable the first few times) or a too-quick recovery (*not* likely the first few times) will mean the same problem shown in Fig. 6-9. You will have to be sure that the nose is not too low at the completion of the half snap and a slight forward pressure may be required to be sure that the airspeed is kept low at the beginning and reasonable at the end of the pull-through. Expect the same type of common errors as listed for the half-aileron-roll entry.

Another variation is a one and one-half snap roll at that position (Fig. 6-10). This maneuver, mentioned here since it is a good follow-up to the reverse Cuban eight, should not be tried by most people until the snap at the top of a loop is well in hand. Needlesss to say, one-and-one-half-snap-roll entries can be an orientation problem at first. In this maneuver, as in the snap at the top of a loop, look to the side in the direction of rotation in order to pick the reference up as soon as possible. Because people tend to look over the nose, the road or railroad reference is seen too late for precise recovery—and a new maneuver is born.

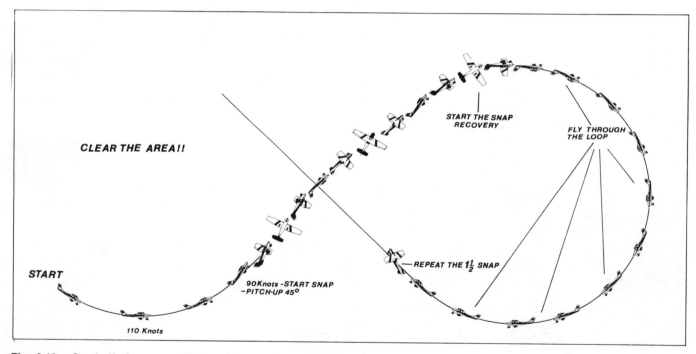

CLEAR THE AREA!!

START THE SNAP RECOVERY

FLY THROUGH THE LOOP

START

90 Knots -START SNAP -PITCH-UP 45°

REPEAT THE 1½ SNAP

110 Knots

Fig. 6-10. One-half of a reverse Cuban eight (one-and-one-half-snap roll entry).

HESITATION ROLLS

THE FOUR-POINT ROLL

Hesitation rolls appear to be the ultimate in aerobatic flying to the beginner, and the eight- and sixteen-point rolls *are* difficult. But the four-point roll can be done reasonably well by a person after 4 or 5 hours of aerobatic instruction.

An entry speed of 120 K (140 mph) is good for the Aerobat; for other aerobatic airplanes without inverted fuel and oil systems you should use the loop speed (or better yet, use the manufacturer's recommended entry speed). Usually, the first few four-point rolls are practiced to the left.

PROCEDURE IN THE FOUR-POINT ROLL. Fig. 6-11, points *1–4,* shows the four-point roll in sequence, and Fig. 6-12, views 1–4, shows the procedure as seen in the cockpit.

After clearing the area, ease the nose down to pick up 120 K. Bring the nose up smoothly to about 20° above the horizon and use left aileron and left rudder to initiate the first 90° roll. At point *1* and view *1,* the ailerons are neutral, right rudder is being held, and the back pressure is relaxed.

Use left aileron and rudder to make the second 90°

roll. The airplane is now inverted. At point *2* and view *2* the ailerons and rudder are neutral with back pressure completely relaxed. Apply full power as the airspeed decreases.

Reapply left aileron and rudder (back pressure relaxed). At point *3* and view *3* the ailerons are neutral; use the left rudder as necessary to stop the nose from dropping during the (very) brief hesitation.

Apply left aileron and left rudder with renewed back pressure as necessary to complete the roll and return to cruise flight.

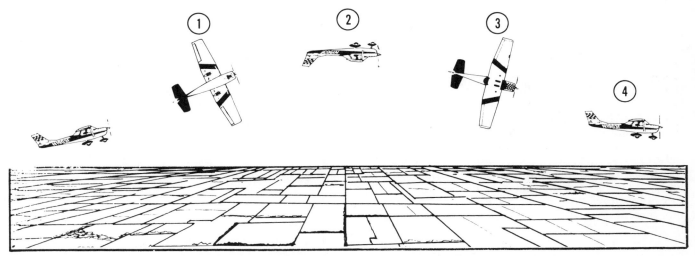

Fig. 6-11. Four-point roll. (See Fig. 6-12 for cockpit views of points *1–4.*) (From *The Flight Instructor's Manual*)

Fig. 6-12. Four-point roll as seen from the cockpit. Views **1–4** would be seen at points *1–4* in Fig. 6-11.

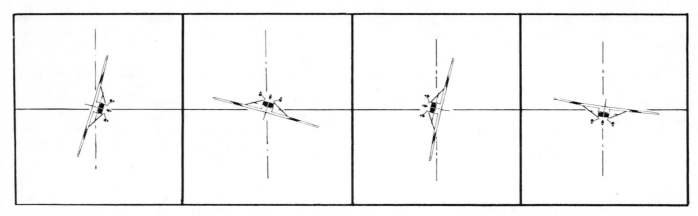

Fig. 6-13. Typical pattern for a trainee's first few four-point aileron rolls. (From *The Flight Instructor's Manual*)

You may prefer to forget about the adding of power the first few times (it could be distracting), but later you'll see that it usually decreases any altitude loss.

For airplanes without inverted fuel and oil systems, the "hesitations" should be short. It's possible to have four good points without the engine hesitating, but the average person will have one problem—being too slow. You might find at first that it's easier to bring the nose up higher (to 30°) in the beginning of the roll so that it can be "falling" throughout the maneuver. Work it so that there is no excess amount of forward pressure used to keep the nose up.

Common Errors in the Four-Point Roll

1. Not stopping precisely at the points. Usually the first point is less than 90° of bank, and the other points are also behind (Fig. 6-13).

2. Having coordination problems—trouble at the first point because of the required use of opposite rudder.

3. Hesitating too long at the first two points so that the rapidly decreasing airspeed (or rapidly lowering nose) makes it necessary to rush the last point.

4. Having poor heading control. This is usually the result of letting the airspeed decay excessively.

THE EIGHT-POINT ROLL

The eight-point roll is an ambitious, but natural, follow-up to the four-point roll. Fig. 6-14 shows the points as they might be remembered. The airplane does not really fly the octagonal pattern shown. It basically rolls *around* a point (an airplane with an inverted system basically rolls *on* a point), but the maneuver is better visualized as an octagon.

The eight-point roll naturally requires better control and a higher airspeed than the four-point. The suggested airspeed for an eight-point roll in the Aerobat is 130 K (150 mph); for other aerobatic airplanes the speed used for the loop plus 10 K can be used as a starter if no recommended speed is given. Usually the problems begin at point *5* in Fig. 6-14, with points *6, 7,*

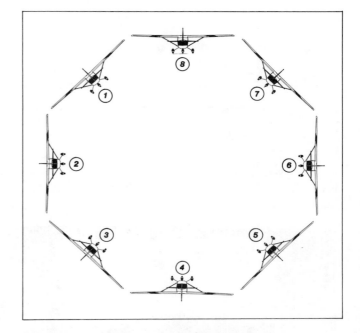

Fig. 6-14. Eight-point roll to the left, depicted as an octagon.

and *8* not so well defined as you hurry to complete the maneuver before it becomes more humorous than precise. Add full power as the airspeed decays.

The common errors of the eight-point roll are those of the four-point roll—only magnified. You'll find that with practice you can get a good eight-point roll with only a brief loss of engine power.

THE REVERSE CLOVERLEAF

The reverse cloverleaf is a more graceful maneuver than the cloverleaf described in Chap. 5. (Some say that the maneuver described in Chap. 5 is the *reverse* cloverleaf, but since this one is more difficult, it would seem to be the variation of the original.)

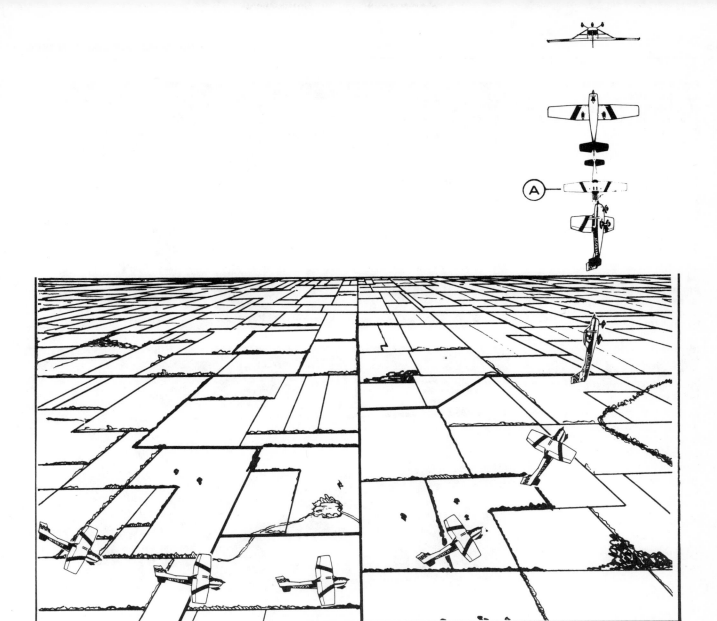

Fig. 6-15. One-fourth of a reverse cloverleaf as seen from above and to the side of the initial dive. Four rolls and four loops complete the maneuver. The four quarter rolls are made in the same direction. (From *The Flight Instructor's Manual*)

In the reverse cloverleaf, the airplane completes the 90° roll while climbing rather than diving. It's still a combination of four loops and four quarter rolls, and the pattern has essentially the same cloverleaf shape when viewed obliquely (Fig. 6-15).

Your ability to maintain orientation will be tested by this one. In the pull-up and roll there is little but sky to be seen (though you will certainly be checking for references on the horizon), so timing and a constant rate of roll are important.

It's suggested, at the beginning anyway, that 130 K (150 mph) be used in the Aerobat for the initial pull-up speed, and with practice you will probably be able to back off to 120 K or the suggested loop entry speed. For other aerobatic airplanes, loop speed plus 10 K might be a good start, with slightly lower speeds being used as

your proficiency improves (of course, you'll use the manufacturer's recommended entry speed, if available).

Throttle handling is like that of other loop-type maneuvers; keep the rpm under the red line at all times.

This maneuver is in one sense a follow-up to the wingover and barrel roll since a wing is placed in line with a point on the horizon when the entry dive is begun. The first part of the reverse cloverleaf is very close to the barrel roll (but the upward path is comparably stretched out).

If possible, in addition to the reference point on the horizon, start the maneuver lined up over a road. Your attitude relative to the road (Fig. 6-15, point *A*) as the airplane is pointed down (and starting to pull through the next loop portion) gives an idea of how the last loop and roll went so you can make minor correc-

Fig. 6-16A-D. Reference road as seen from the cockpit at each part of the loop with the pitch attitude at point *A* in Fig. 6-15. The arrows indicate the direction of the initial dive and pull-up.

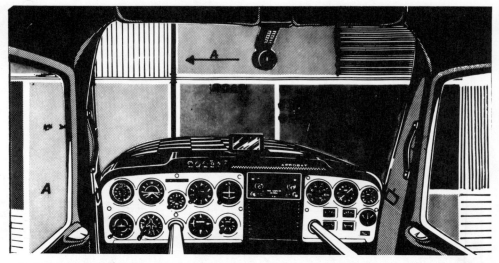

(A) The backside of the first loop, the airplane's pull-up perpendicular to the road (it was lined up with it in the initial dive, as indicated by the arrow).

(B) The backside of the second loop, the airplane again lined up with the reference road but the heading 180° from that of the initial dive.

tions as necessary for the next part (Fig. 6-16A–D). If you are rolling to the *left* in the upward portion of the maneuver, the airplane will have turned 90° to the *right* each time the nose is headed vertically down at the road system. The points on the horizon off the wing tip have to be quickly chosen as each dive is entered, and since chances are small that there will be four outstanding references at positions perpendicular to, or in line with, the road, you may have disorientation problems.

Your instructor will initially have you practice only one part, adding the rest as your proficiency (and orientation) improves.

Fig. 6-17 shows the horizon reference at the initial dive and as the roll portion is completed. Unlike the barrel roll, *here* the roll portion is stopped when the wings are level (inverted) and the nose is pointed at the reference. The nose is brought smoothly (wings-level) through the point and the road reference is picked up.

The most precise form of the maneuver is a "true" reverse cloverleaf with the airplane completing exactly 90° of *roll* while its nose is straight up, then back pres-

sure applied to fly through the loop portion. However, more practically in lower-powered trainers (such as the Aerobat), the roll and loop are combined to make sure that it's not a situation of running out of airspeed, altitude, and inspiration before the maneuver gets a good start. Use a smooth continual motion of loop and roll.

In this suggested procedure for the Aerobat (and other lower-powered aerobatic airplanes), back pressure is used as the roll is made, which helps "turn" the nose toward the point. The usual tendency is to turn *more* than 90° from the original heading—having turned past the point when the airplane reaches the wings-level position (Fig. 6–18).

In the situation shown in Fig. 6-18, *left* rudder may be used to yaw the nose back to the point, as was discussed for the reverse Cuban eight. Of course, this is supposed to be a reasonably coordinated maneuver (and with practice it will be a fully coordinated one); however, you might salvage a slipup by subtle use of rudder.

Continual back pressure should be used, and there

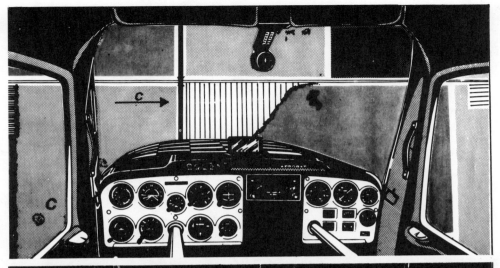

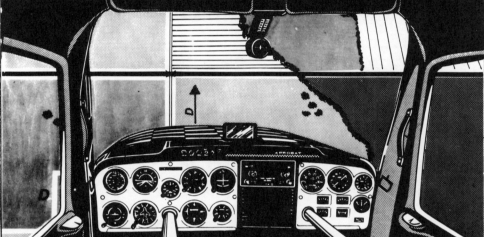

(C) The backside of the third loop, the pull-up path again perpendicular to the reference road (but in a reverse direction from view **A**).

(D) The backside of the fourth loop, the airplane being pulled up to level flight and headed in the same direction as at the beginning of the maneuver.

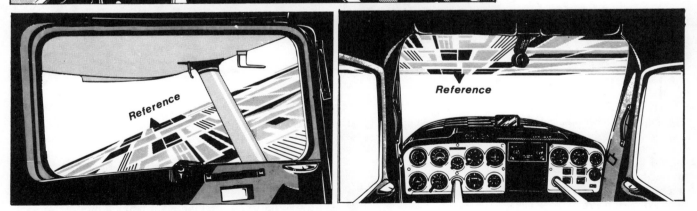

Fig. 6-17. Reference for the reverse cloverleaf as seen from the Aerobat.

Fig. 6-18. View from the cockpit when the airplane has turned more than 90° from the original heading, overshooting the reference. (If this picture looks backward, get a model and exaggerate the turn in the pull-up and left roll.)

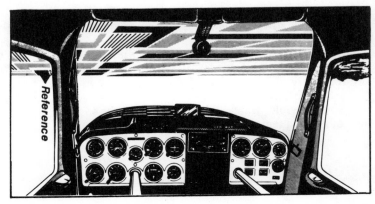

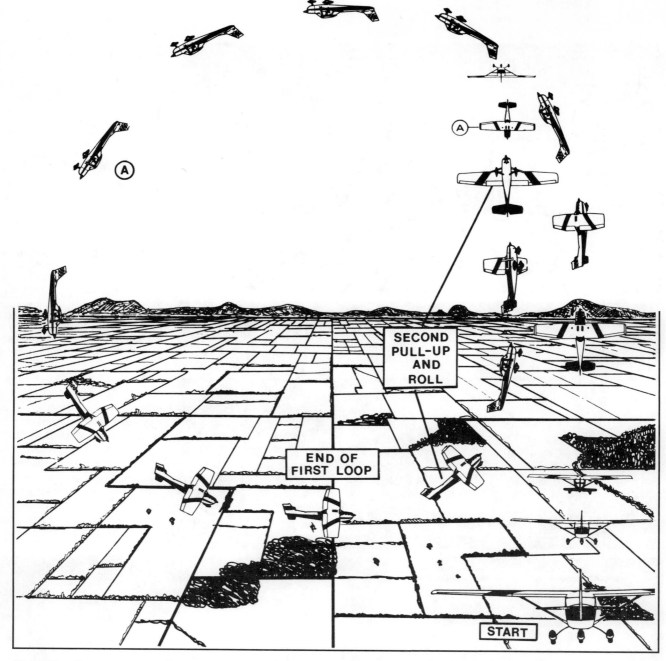

Fig. 6-19. Reverse cloverleaf viewed from behind the initial dive. (From *The Flight Instructor's Manual*)

should be no hesitation or stopping of the nose at the inverted position. A slight relaxation of back pressure at about 30° above the horizon, though, will give the loop portion more symmetry.

One common error is using too much back pressure throughout the top half of the loop portion and not enough at the bottom, resulting in high airspeed and excessive loss of altitude.

You can see errors in "pull" or roll when the road reference comes back into view. By doing only one loop and roll portion at first, you'll be able to stop and analyze your problems.

Some people "gain" a heading of nearly 45° per unit of the maneuver and wonder why, when it's com-

pleted, they are headed almost 180° from the original heading. This can add to any disorientation for a few seconds after completion of the full maneuver.

By analyzing the maneuver using a model, you will find that the airplane's attitude at a particular point of the action can later affect its path in a manner that's not always predictable—without prior analysis.

Fig. 6-19 shows a part of the reverse cloverleaf. The second pull-up and roll has been moved slightly in for viewing purposes. You, of course, will fly the airplane in such a manner that the second pull-up and roll would be exactly in line. The two points marked *A* correspond to the attitude shown in Fig. 6-15.

7

RECOVERIES FROM UNUSUAL ATTITUDES

WAKE TURBULENCE

As noted in Chapter 1, many people take an aerobatic course not in order to go on to competing or doing airshows but to add a safety factor to their general flying. They think that perhaps such training will give them a better chance for survival, as for instance, in a wake turbulence encounter. Aerobatic training *does* give you a better chance of recovery (given enough altitude), but don't think that after such a course wake turbulence will no longer be considered a dangerous situation, even if you turn out to be the world's greatest aerobatic ace. If wake turbulence from one wide-body jet can upset another wide-body, you would have quite a ride in a four-place family airplane (or any other general aviation airplane). And smaller airplanes have their own wake turbulence, too.

Several factors are working against you when encountering wake turbulence:

1. *Surprise*—You've been aware of possible wake turbulence problems at every takeoff and landing for the past 5 years, but the one time you are distracted on landing (or takeoff) is when you get involved with it.

2. *Slow airspeed*—The airspeed will be slower while taking off and landing (when *control effectiveness = deflection × CAS* becomes evident). The curve in Fig. 7-1 for a fictitious airplane is generally true for most airplanes. As you can see, the rate of roll at the approach speed is considerably less than the maximum, and adding the low power and dirty condition on approach makes the rate of roll low indeed.

3. *Low altitude*—It goes without saying that an airplane is low during takeoff and landing, which can lead to a fatal accident because of loss of control in a wake turbulence encounter. (At altitude and at cruise and higher airspeeds, structural damage might be the deciding factor.)

4. *Dirty configuration*—The airplane will have the gear and flaps down for landing, and the gear and (for some types) flaps may be down for takeoff. The drag of gear and flaps slows the acceleration needed to get out of the situation.

5. *Low power*—Certainly on *approach* the power will be well reduced. This is a bad situation for suddenly having to recover and avoid hitting the ground.

6. *Front-seat passenger*—If an airplane is upset by wake turbulence, so are the persons in the airplane. The person in the right seat will grab onto something—and what is a better handle than the control wheel placed by the designer so conveniently in front of him or her? Most passengers will *pull* on the wheel, particularly if the airplane is inverted (or nearly so); when an airplane is inverted, *pulling* on the control wheel is an action you'd rather do without. In a situation like this, the occupant of the right front seat usually turns out to be (1) a King Kong, (2) an opera soprano hitting some high C's in your right ear, or (3) a King Kong whose voice, under the existing conditions, shifts several octaves higher, giving you the benefit of *both* physical strength and volume.

Your instructor may demonstrate, and have you practice, recoveries from inverted attitudes that are deliberately set up; you will use full power and "push and roll" to get back upright with the least altitude loss.

Add full power as the roll is started, and *push* and roll. Keep the aileron and rudder in. As the airplane rolls upright, use back pressure. (The Immelmann is a good maneuver for the introduction of rolling upright from a wake turbulence upset—see Chap. 5). Airplanes without an inverted fuel system will lose power as you push and roll.

Probably your first reaction when rolled inverted will be to let the nose drop, or even to perform the second half of a loop, losing several hundred feet. After a few tries you'll probably limit the altitude loss to

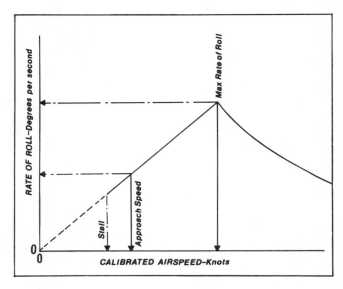

Fig. 7-1. Rate of roll versus airspeed for a fictitious airplane. This is the general form of any roll-rate/velocity curve for an airplane with unboosted controls.

perhaps 300 ft. (Think about that a little—you are primed and ready for it but still will lose 300 or 400 ft. Figure the altitude loss in a situation 3 or 4 years from now when your recovery technique has gotten rusty and you're surprised.)

The instructor may next have you roll *opposite* to the original roll, not because you would necessarily do this in a real situation, but because this would require initiation of a roll recovery, not just carrying on what the instructor started.

There's a good argument for your rolling *with* the turbulence-induced roll. If the vortex is powerful enough to get the airplane inverted before you can stop it, you might *lock* the airplane in that condition by trying to roll against it. One instructor indicated (tongue-in-cheek) that it would be better to make a sloppy roll to get out of the vortex (a precision roll may cause the airplane to stay in the core) and during the process turn toward the control tower so the folks in there can share your excitement.

In practicing recoveries, the instructor may pick an altitude as "ground level," do a half roll at about 400 ft above that reference, and have you recover from it. You'll find that on occasion you'll use more than the altitude allowed, which brings up the point that you won't have a lot of luck with wake turbulence at lower altitudes with all the factors (surprise, slow, low, etc.) working against you. (This recovery practice could be the final factor that convinces you wake turbulence is to be avoided at *all* costs.)

HOOD WORK

Aileron Rolls under the Hood. The instructor can introduce *hooded* recoveries by starting off with aileron rolls under the hood. Fig. 7-2A–H, drawn from a series of photos taken during an aileron roll, shows the instrument readings for the Aerobat and other airplanes equipped with a 360°-roll attitude indicator during the steps of the maneuver.

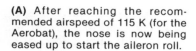

Fig. 7-2 A-H. Readings on the airspeed indicator, attitude indicator, and altimeter during an aileron roll.

(A) After reaching the recommended airspeed of 115 K (for the Aerobat), the nose is now being eased up to start the aileron roll.

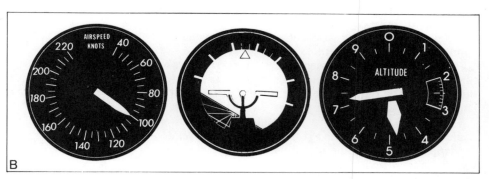

(B) When the pitch-up attitude of 30° is attained, an aileron roll is started to the left.

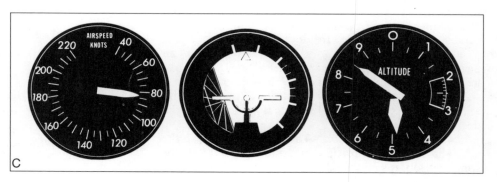

(C) The roll continues, and altitude is still being gained.

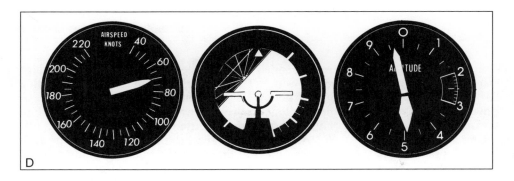

(D) The back pressure is being relaxed as the airspeed reaches a minimum of 70 K.

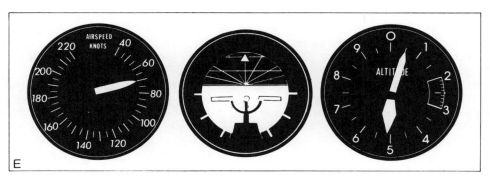

(E) The airplane is exactly inverted at minimum airspeed (70 K) and maximum altitude.

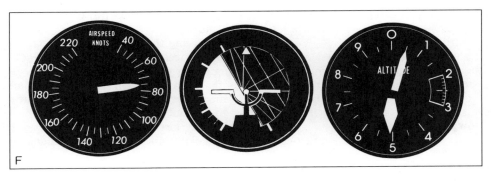

(F) As the roll continues past inverted, the altitude is at the peak and the airspeed is increasing.

(G) Back pressure and left rudder pressure are increased as the roll approaches completion.

(H) The roll is complete at a constant altitude and airspeed.

For recovering under the hood in the Aerobat (or other aerobatic airplanes with similar instruments), an attitude indicator is the primary aid. The procedure is the same as without the hood (add power and roll), with the idea of keeping the airplane pip in the instrument above the horizon at first, then bringing it on the horizon as the roll is completed. (You wouldn't practice this solo—a safety pilot is needed for hood work.)

The airplane may still contact the ground, but the point is to have any contact *right side up*. Again, remember that *no aerobatic training can guarantee recovery from a wake turbulence upset*.

Review the wake turbulence information in the *Airman's Information Manual* and get copies of FAA AC 90-23, an advisory circular on wake turbulence.

Common Errors in Roll Recoveries—Visual and Hooded

1. Letting the nose drop when the airplane is inverted at the initiation of the recovery roll.

2. Not adding power as the recovery is started.

3. Neutralizing ailerons during the recovery (see the common errors in the aileron roll listed in Chap. 4).

4. Making a *too-slow* roll—the nose drops during the roll with an unallowable altitude loss.

5. Applying too-enthusiastic forward pressure and *little roll*—pinning the occupants against the belts and harness with, again, too much altitude loss during the final part of the recovery (a half loop sometimes results).

6. Neglecting to apply back pressure as the roll is completed—the nose ends up too low and altitude is unnecessarily lost.

Loops under the Hood.
Depending on how far you plan to go with the recoveries from unusual attitudes, you might want to do a couple of hooded loops in the Aerobat (with the instructor briefing you).

Doing aerobatic maneuvers under the hood requires close and quick instrument scanning, which can help your day-to-day instrument flying. (Making a steady-state climb or descent is easier after you've done some loops and rolls under the hood.)

Keep the wings level with the attitude indicator (A/I) and ease the nose down to pick up 120 K (or the recommended loop airspeed for the aerobatic airplane you're using). Then smoothly bring the nose up, with a pull of about 3.5 g's, continuing the back pressure as the airplane proceeds toward the inverted position. Smoothly open the throttle to full power.

As the airplane reaches the vertical nose-up position, the horizon line in the attitude indicator will *roll* 180° (it's supposed to), so that as the airplane flies over on its back the ground and sky portions of the A/I are in their proper positions. Relax the back pressure slightly as the airplane reaches the 30°-nose-up (inverted) position.

Check the wings for level as the airplane is in the full inverted position at the top of the loop.

Start increasing the back pressure slightly as the nose reaches the 30°-nose-down point on the back side of the loop.

As the airplane reaches the vertical nose-down position, the attitude indicator will again *roll* 180°, putting the ground and sky indications of the A/I in the proper positions. Reduce power.

Smoothly continue the pullout (with wings level) and level off, using the A/I. Adjust power when level cruising flight is attained.

Basically, you're doing the same loop you've practiced with outside references (except you won't be looking out at the wing tip as you pull up). After a few of these you'll see the idea and will be getting some smooth, precise maneuvers. The instructor will naturally be keeping an eye out for other airplanes.

The instructor may also demonstrate and let you practice some Cuban eights and Immelmanns under the hood.

Inverted Recoveries under the Hood—A Summary.
Fig. 7-3A–E shows some steps in recovering from an inverted position. At Fig. 7-3A, full power is added. Forward pressure is used to hold the nose "up" to minimize altitude loss (Fig. 7-3B). (Forget the comfort of your passengers—they should have had their belts tight anyway.) Fig. 7-3C shows that the roll (to the right in this case) is continued, keeping the reference pip at or slightly above the horizon. In Fig. 7-3D, the pip has moved below the horizon. Back pressure should be

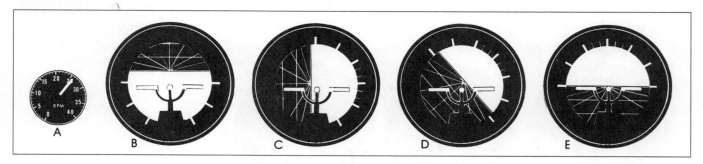

Fig. 7-3. Instrument readings during an inverted recovery. **(A)** Fuil power added here. **(B)** Forward pressure applied here. **(C)** The reference pip should be kept slightly above the horizon. (Keep the pip "in the blue" or as close to the blue [sky] portion of the face as possible.) **(D)** Back pressure added. **(E)** Recovery completed.

applied to keep the nose up. At the completion (Fig. 7-3E), the airplane is wings-level and in a level-pitch attitude.

After a practice recovery, the instructor might start another roll (after again clearing the area). In an actual encounter, however, you may prefer to ask the tower for another runway rather than roll again.

Spin Recoveries under the Hood. Fig. 7-4 shows the partial panel instrument indications in a developed left spin in an Aerobat. (It's assumed here that the flaps are up when doing deliberate spinning.)

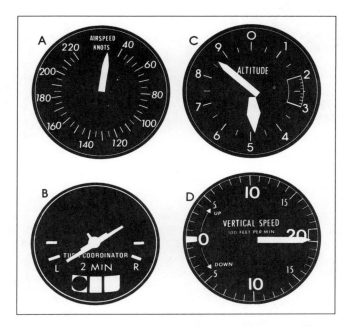

Fig. 7-4. Indications of the partial (emergency) panel instruments (pilot's side) in a developed left spin in an Aerobat (and some other side-by-side airplanes). **(A)** The airspeed is very low. **(B)** The turn coordinator airplane or the turn and slip needle is indicating a left yaw. **(C)** The altimeter is showing a rapid loss of altitude. **(D)** The vertical speed indicator is pegged —down.

To recover (the steps are also shown in Fig. 3-9):
Make sure the throttle is fully closed.
Neutralize the ailerons.
Get the flaps up if an inadvertent spin occurs with them down. There are two reasons for this: (1) the maximum flaps-extended speed (V_{FE}) may be exceeded during the recovery and (2) for some airplanes, extended flaps may cause the nose to pitch up and tend to make the spin go flat.
Apply full rudder opposite to the small airplane in the turn coordinator or the needle in the turn and slip. The ball in the instruments in the Aerobat and some

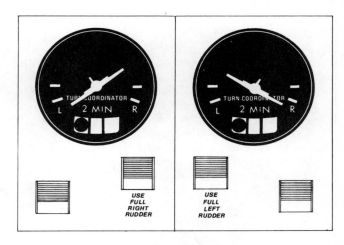

Fig. 7-5. Check the turn coordinator or turn and slip in spin recoveries. Apply full opposite rudder to the needle or small airplane indication.

other side-by-side airplanes will always be to the *left* for left *or* right spins (instrument on the pilot's side) (Fig. 7-5).

Immediately after applying full rudder, move the control wheel forward. Be prepared to pull it back if you overdid the briskness and get light in your seat. Check the airspeed for an *increase* from the very low (sometimes zero) indication. This is a sign that the recovery has started (Fig. 7-6). The turn coordinator has considerable damping and will lag in indicating the ces-

Fig. 7-6. After applying full opposite rudder and moving the wheel briskly forward, the airspeed moving from the zero or near-zero indication shows that the recovery has started. Neutralize the rudder and start applying back pressure to pull out of the dive.

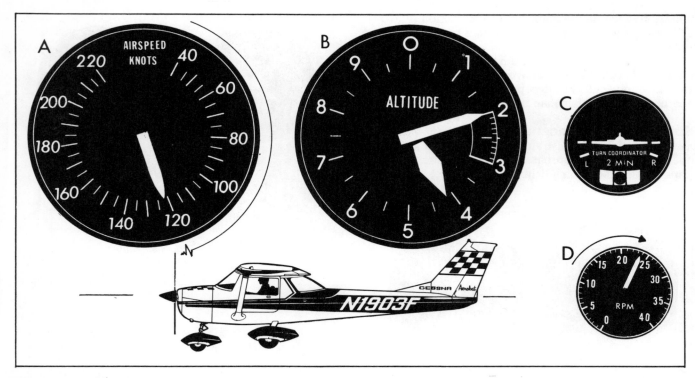

Fig. 7-7. Steps and instrument indications in the latter part of the spin recovery (from the dive to the return to level cruising flight).

sation of roll and yaw, and the nose may be held down too long with a too-high airspeed and extra loss of altitude during the pullout, so don't depend on it during this stage of the recovery.

When the airspeed starts increasing, neutralize the rudder and start pulling out of the dive.

Compare the following items with Fig. 7-7.

During the pullout from the dive when the airspeed makes a change—it stops increasing, or decreases, from its indication (say, in the vicinity of 120 K)—the nose is approximately level (Fig. 7-7A). Relax the back pressure.

Check the altimeter and "fly" the particular altitude noted at the point of nose-level attitude (Fig. 7-7B).

Now you can keep the wings level with the turn coordinator or turn and slip (Fig. 7-7C).

As the airspeed reduces to cruise, apply cruise power (Fig. 7-7D).

Incidentally, there are a couple of instrument indications in addition to those just discussed that will show whether the Aerobat is in an upright spin or a spiral.

In a tight spiral the accelerometer shows that higher-than-1-g forces are acting on the airplane and pilot. Fig. 7-8 shows the accelerometer indications in an Aerobat in one developed spin. The "inert" hands have been moved to show that the working hand maintained a constant +1 g after the spin stabilized. The accelero-

Fig. 7-8. Accelerometer indications throughout a steady-state, developed spin in Aerobat N7557L. You may find that in some spins in your airplane the accelerometer may show slightly higher readings.

meter in the Aerobat is close to the center of gravity.

Another indication for the Aerobat (and it may apply to other airplanes as well) is that in a stabilized spin the fuel gages indicate considerably less fuel because centrifugal force is "unporting" both fuel tanks, causing the fuel to move outward away from the floats in the tanks. As an example, a developed spin in the Aerobat with the tanks half full resulted in an indication of zero fuel in both tanks throughout the stabilized spin. A developed spin with tanks full gave an indication of roughly one-half fuel during the stabilized portion. Balanced-turn, tight spirals result in fuel indications of relative accuracy. (Not that you'll be checking the fuel volume in the middle of a spin *or* a spiral — this may only be trivia, but the book can't be dull and technical all of the time.)

Common Errors in Spin Recoveries under the Hood

1. Failing to close the throttle and/or neutralize the ailerons before starting the recovery.

2. Not noticing that the recovery has started and letting the airspeed get too high before starting the pull-out.

3. Holding opposite rudder *after* the rotation has stopped.

4. Failing to note the indications of nose-level attitude and pulling the nose up too high. (This might allow practice of another spin, perhaps in the opposite direction.)

SUMMARY

The maneuvers and recoveries in this chapter were discussed to give you a look at some procedures not normally encountered in flight courses or textbooks. (The hooded *spiral* recovery was not included because it is well covered in flight courses and books.) The aerobatic course you are taking may not cover any of the procedures dealt with here, but remembering these steps might sometime help you out of a bind in your everyday flying. Do *not* practice these maneuvers except in an airplane certificated for them with an instructor who is qualified to instruct them.

BIBLIOGRAPHY

Listed here are books suggested for further reading:

Cessna Aircraft Company. 1969. *Cessna 150 Aerobat Training Manual*. Wichita: Cessna Aircraft Co.
Cole, Duane. 1965. *Roll around a Point*. Milwaukee: Ken Cook Co.
_____. 1970. *Conquest of Lines and Symmetry*. Milwaukee: Ken Cook Transnational.
Callier, Debbie Gary. 1978. *Pilot Proficiency Training Manual*. Alexandria, Minn.: Bellanca Aircraft Corp.
Kershner, William K. 1981. *The Flight Instructor's Manual*. 2d ed. Ames: Iowa State University Press.
Mason, Sammy. 1985. *Stalls, Spins and Safety*. New York: Macmillan.
Medore, Art. 1970. *Primary Aerobatic Flight Training with Military Techniques*. Dover, N.J.: Ardot Enterprises, Inc.
O'Dell, Bob. 1980. *Aerobatics Today*. New York: St. Martin's Press.
Smith, Robert T. 1980. *Advanced Flight Maneuvers and Aerobatics*. Blue Ridge Summit, Pa.: Tab Books.
Williams, Neil. 1975. *Aerobatics*. Shrewsbury, Eng.: Airlife Publ.

S Y L L A B U S

This syllabus comprises 5 hours of ground school
and 5 hours of dual instruction.

FIRST FLIGHT

GROUND INSTRUCTION (1:00)

___1. Discussion of the course, aims, and general procedures. (Always clear the area before starting any aerobatic maneuver.)

___2. Discussion of the effects of g forces on the airplane and pilot.

___3. Discussion of limit load factors (g's) of normal ($+3.8$, -1.52), utility ($+4.4$, -1.76), and aerobatic ($+6.0$, -3.0) airplanes. (Why aerobatics should not be done in normal or utility airplanes.)

___4. Discussion of probable g forces to be encountered in the course ($+4$, 0). (How the accelerometer works.)

___5. Discussion of pilot physiology. (How to avoid or cope with nausea problems by stopping at the first "loss of enthusiasm"—the It's Not So Much Fun Anymore Syndrome—staying up in smooth air versus immediately returning to the airport, and avoiding certain types of food or drink before flying aerobatics.)

___6. Discussion of introductory or review maneuvers and common errors.
   ___a. The 1-g stall (power-on).
   ___b. The 720° constant-altitude steep turns (45° or 60° banks).
   ___c. The chandelle, as a maneuver introductory to aerobatics and as required for the commercial certificate.
   ___d. The wingover (60°, then vertical banks at the steepest point).
   ___e. The lazy eight, as a series of shallow wingovers and as required for the commercial certificate.

___7. Introduction of the aileron roll (one of the Three Fundamentals of aerobatics).
   ___a. Procedure (the maneuver as a whole, power setting and airspeeds).
   ___b. Breaking the maneuver into the usage of each control.
   ___c. The aileron roll again as a whole maneuver.
   ___d. The left and right aileron roll with expected differences in effects of "torque."
   ___e. Common errors.

___8. Preflight check of the airplane with special emphasis on checking for any structural damage.

___9. Briefing at the airplane concerning the parachute and procedure in exiting the airplane.

FLIGHT (0:45)

___1. Climb to a safe altitude in a clear area. Instructor shows trainee practice area limits.

___2. Demonstration and practice of 720° turns (45° and 60° banks).

___3. Demonstration and practice of chandelles (30° initial bank) and wingovers (60° and 90° banks).

___4. Demonstration and practice of aileron rolls. Trainee does at least two left rolls and one right roll.

___5. Postflight briefing and critique of maneuvers.

Comments _____

_____

_____

_____

_____

_____

Instructor_____

Date_____ Ground School_____ Flight Time_____

SECOND FLIGHT

GROUND INSTRUCTION (1:00)

___1. Review of chandelles and wingovers.

___2. Review of the aileron roll (techniques and common errors).

___3. Introduction of the loop as the second Fundamental—the maneuver as a whole, step-by-step procedure, and common errors.

___4. Discussion of the loop followed by an aileron roll.

___5. Introduction of the cloverleaf as a simple combination of the two Fundamentals, and common errors.

___6. Introduction of the Cuban eight as the next combination of the two Fundamentals.

___7. Brief discussion of spin entries and recoveries.

FLIGHT (0:45)

___ 1. Aileron rolls (left and right).

___ 2. Demonstration and practice of loops with instructor handling throttle.

___ 3. Practice of loops with trainee handling throttle.

___ 4. Loops followed by aileron rolls with instructor, then trainee, handling throttle.

___ 5. Instructor demonstrates one or two parts of cloverleaf.

___ 6. Trainee practices cloverleaf with instructor handling throttle.

___ 7. Instructor demonstrates one-half of Cuban eight.

___ 8. Trainee practices Cuban eights with instructor handling throttle.

___ 9. Instructor demonstrates hands-off spin recovery at two turns.

___10. Trainee does a hands-off recovery at two turns followed by a three-turn left spin and standard recovery.

___11. Postflight review.

Comments _____

_____

_____

_____

_____

_____

Instructor_____

Date_____ Ground School_____ Flight Time_____

THIRD FLIGHT

GROUND INSTRUCTION (0:45)

___1. Review of aileron rolls, loops, Cuban eights, and spins.
___2. Discussion of spin theory (airplane spin certification, factors that affect spin characteristics).
___3. Discussion of spins to be practiced at end of flight (at least one three-turn spin in each direction).
___4. Discussion of the Immelmann, as a next step in the loop-roll combination and as an introduction to recoveries from inverted flight.

FLIGHT (0:45)

___1. Practice of aileron rolls left and right.
___2. Loops followed by aileron rolls with the trainee handling throttle.
___3. Practice of Cuban eights with trainee handling throttle.
___4. Demonstration and practice of the Immelmann.
___5. Practice of a three-turn spin in each direction.
___6. Postflight review.

Comments _____

_____

_____

_____

_____

_____

Instructor_____

Date_____ Ground School_____ Flight Time_____

FOURTH FLIGHT

GROUND INSTRUCTION (0:45)

___1. Discussion of airplane certification and categories.
___2. Discussion of maneuvering and gust envelopes and airspeed indicator markings.
___3. Discussion of the effects of airplane weight on maneuvering speed.
___4. Discussion of the effects of weight on the reactions of the airplane to vertical gusts.
___5. Review of normal stalls and introduction of accelerated stalls.
___6. Review of spins with a discussion of various entries.
___7. Review of Cuban eight.
___8. Introduction of the snap roll as a "horizontal spin."
___9. Discussion of snaps at the top of a loop.

FLIGHT (0:45)

___1. Practice of cloverleafs and Cuban eights.
___2. Demonstration and practice of snap rolls.
___3. Practice of spins with over-the-top, under-the-bottom, and normal entries (at least one entry of each type).
___4. Demonstration (and practice) of a snap at the top of a loop.
___5. Postflight review.

Comments _____

_____

_____

_____

_____

_____

Instructor_____

Date_____ Ground School_____ Flight Time_____

FIFTH FLIGHT

GROUND INSTRUCTION (0:45)

___1. Discussion of longitudinal stability, static and dynamic.
___2. Discussion of the FAR requirement for stability.
___3. Discussion of forces and moments on an airplane in flight.
___4. Discussion of weight and balance effects on longitudinal stability.
___5. Discussion of the ground effect (takeoff and landing performance and stability).
___6. Review of aileron roll, loop, snap roll, and Cuban eight.
___7. Discussion of wake turbulence and methods of recovery. (Avoidance is the best policy because no aerobatic course can ensure a successful recovery. Emphasis on *roll* rather than split-S, or half-loop, recovery.)
___8. Discussion of aileron roll, loop, and spin recoveries under the hood.

FLIGHT (1:00)

___1. Warm-up with loop, aileron roll, and snap combination.
___2. Practice of one or more Cuban eights.
___3. Demonstration of the airplane's longitudinal stability.
___4. Demonstration and practice of half-roll recoveries from wake turbulence upsets, rolls with and against initial upset to compare effectiveness of recovery and altitude loss.
___5. Practice of aileron rolls and loops under the hood (optional).
___6. Recovery from inverted flight under the hood (optional).
___7. Practice of spin recovery under the hood (optional).
___8. Postflight review.

Comments _____

_____

_____

_____

_____

_____

Instructor_____

Date_____ Ground School_____ Flight Time_____

SIXTH FLIGHT

GROUND INSTRUCTION (0:45)

___1. Introduction of the barrel roll, reviewing the wingover.
___2. Discussion of the four-point roll (optional).
___3. Description of reverse Cuban eights, eight-point roll, and reverse cloverleaf (optional).
___4. Effects on spin of aileron use and of power. (Why the ailerons should be neutral and the throttle closed for the most effective recovery.)
___5. Review of maneuvers covered in course (as requested by trainee).
  ___a. Aileron roll.
  ___b. Loop.
  ___c. Cloverleaf.
  ___d. Cuban eight.
  ___e. Immelmann.
  ___f. Snap roll.
  ___g. Spin.

FLIGHT (1:00)

Review and practice of as many of the briefed maneuvers as time allows, with special emphasis on spins, including demonstration of power and pro- and antispin ailerons on rotation rate and recovery.

Comments _____

_____

_____

_____

_____

_____

Instructor_____

Date_____ Ground School_____ Flight Time_____

I N D E X